Gray Matters

Proper Care and Feeding of a Weimaraner "Owner"

Ken Moore

MooreGrayMatters.com

Contents

Introduction - I Am Duped by Women and Weimaraners

Every once in a while, there was some chatter around our house about getting a dog. My wife wanted a hunting dog and the preferred breed was a Weimaraner. That sounded okay to me, I'd seen pictures of them and they look really cool. But, in that chatter I was also picking up caveats and thinly veiled warnings about these dogs. Weimaraner's are time intensive, she said. They can take over your life, she said. We'd never be able to handle one, especially now when things are already so crazy. I'd already heard they were high maintenance dogs and needed constant attention but she was acting like we were getting a buffalo or a herd of yaks. It's just a dog right? Feed it, walk it, pet it, right?

I marvel at the level of my utter cluelessness. My wife remained the voice of reason and called the whole thing off. We, meaning me, weren't ready for a Weimaraner. And if we couldn't get the kind of dog she wanted, then we wouldn't get one at all.

So, we weren't getting a dog, and definitely not one of those crazy ones. We were making the smart responsible decision. We weren't ready for such a major commitment and we knew it. "That's fine", I said, maybe we'll get one when life is less hectic. Maybe after we retire. I then settled into a worry free, no dog existence. My time was my own, my commitments few. And then somehow, when I wasn't looking, I was tricked into getting a Weimaraner.

Suddenly, all the concerns we once had were brushed aside. We'd deal with whatever came up and it would be worth it right? Sure, I said, still blissfully unaware. How much trouble could it really be? Later I thought, this dog should come with a caution label that says: Warning, I'm a lot of trouble. I had just been enrolled in Weimaraner school and was about to learn the difference between a Weimaraner and a "normal" dog.

I did have one reason to suspect that Weimaraner's were different than other dogs. My only previous experience with these dogs was being bitten by one in a liquor store. Never mind what I was doing in the store. What happened is that I reached out to open a cooler door, a Weimaraner that I'd never seen before ran down the aisle, bit me lightly on the hand, and then continued on it's way. It ran down the aisle and skittered around the corner out of sight. I never saw it again. I hadn't thought of this liquor store Weimaraner in years. But, I remembered it when I found myself trying to figure how my life had become overrun by a mere dog. Our Weimaraner was always up to some foolishness. Then I realized that if a Weimaraner could work security in a liquor store, it could certainly trick me into doing whatever it wanted.

From the beginning I was skeptical of the notion that getting a dog would improve our lives. I liked our life the way it was, complications don't usually make things better. But, I didn't know what our lives were lacking. I certainly didn't think a dog would change our lives in as many ways as it did. What I remembered about the dogs I've had before is that there's a lot of responsibility. And a lot of picking up poop. I guess I was hoping, in some vague way, that a Weimaraner would be fun.

Although I had received some advanced warning that Weimaraner's brought more "energy" to the table than most other dogs, I thought I was prepared for what I was getting into. I envisioned longer than normal walks and a little more play time. But, Sadie was a bigger personality than I had imagined a dog could be. She soon had us wrapped up in her Weimaraner web and "Life before Sadie" was a dimly remembered memory.

Sadie has an enthusiasm for everything that is infectious. She turns mundane tasks into adventures. Everything is an event now. Changing a light bulb is a project and a chance for her to supervise my every move. Every person that walks by the yard is a potential robber. Every squirrel is a threat to the integrity of our bird feeder. She never tires of sending them scurrying up trees. Opening the front door is an electrifying experience. Crinkle a bag and watch the sparks fly. Fail to pay attention to her and she stomps her foot at you. She brings more effort and style to catching a rubber ball than is necessary, or normal. Just catching the ball is not enough, adding a degree of difficulty keeps things interesting. A leap with a half twist behind the back catch is a favorite. She's thinking way too much about catching the ball, clearly.

That's not all that was included with the purchase of our first Weimaraner. Sadie is more focused on the people around her than any dog I've ever seen. She takes an interest in everything you are doing. That includes everything. There's a lot of eye contact and tail wagging going on. Whatever you want to do, she's in. She's also a snuggly dog. Her preferred place to take a nap is right up next to you. It's easy to get attached to a dog that wants to be your nap buddy.

She has a way of making people happy to take care of her and give her what she wants. Sadie knows it only takes a minute of the sad eye, wiggle butt, and face lick routine to melt the average dog lover's heart. That explains why they get so attached to her. It's a version of mind control. She instinctively brings people under her spell. We started referring to "Sadie's public" when she was very young. Just a few seconds of exposure to her charms turns strangers into friends.

I also noticed her doing things my previous dogs didn't do. Little things like luring me out of my chair so she can steal it. This happened a number of times before I could be sure she was consciously doing it. On a walk in the field she likes to run straight at me and zig zag right in front of me close enough to make me stop walking. She does this just to scare me into thinking she's going to crash into me. And no matter what I tell myself, it always works. She also does weird stuff like swimming across the bed and batting the door stop spring when she wants to go out. These things started to pile up until I started to think that there was something to these Weimaraner's that was really special.

I'm not the first person to notice these special qualities in Weimaraners. I remember seeing a magazine article from the 1950's that said Weimaraner's think they are people and that they will answer the phone. These kinds of exaggerations led to an explosion of impulse Weimaraner buying that almost ruined the breed. Fortunately, none of those old myths are true. The truth is crazy enough, there's no need to exaggerate.

I don't believe that Sadie has some complex theory about life. But, she's got something that makes her seize the day the way I'd like to. Watching the way her whole body vibrates when I come home made me wonder why she is so much happier to see me than I am to see her. I'm not psychoanalyzing her or trying to read her mind. I just want to be so happy that I can't stop shaking my tail. There should be a way of tapping into that happiness without scientifically deconstructing her behavior.

The problem with most dog books is that often the dog dies at the end. I read that book Marley and Me and felt like my own dog had died. Sorry if you didn't know that Marley dies at the end of that book. It seems to be a time tested formula but it wears me out. The dog book buying public seems to be tougher in this area than I am.

I don't know if I'll be able to write about our dogs after they die. So, I decided to do it now, when they are in their prime and causing trouble on a daily basis. No dogs die in this book, that's not the part of dog owning I'm interested in.

Weimaraner history includes both a secret origin and a period of wild popularity. Both of these episodes allude to the fact that people go crazy for these dogs. I don't know of any other breeds that were kept secret from "commoners". And I can't name any that became popular so quickly that the breed was literally in danger of losing its hunting instincts.

Many people have a perception about Weimaraner's that comes from unrealistic expectations based on those old exaggerated stories. The feeling is that these dogs are all show and no hunt. In hunting circles, Weimaraner's are often misunderstood and underestimated. Attitudes take a long time to change, especially when people are convinced that what they think they know is the truth. Exploring these perceptions has been a lot of fun for me. I'm not so sure I can change these attitudes with a few stories about our dogs. Ultimately, the Weimaraner's themselves will change more people than any book. As more people are exposed to them in a hunting environment, word starts to spread.

I knew that Sadie was an exceptionally bright dog. Still, she's just one dog. I couldn't expect all Weimaraner's to be like her. Then we got Grace, who confirmed for me that Weimaraner's are a rare breed. She's the bossiest, pushiest dog to ever try to become leader of my pack. Grace was like this right out of the box. We didn't screw up her instructions. She's what you would call, a dominant dog. She's what she would call, your leader. The day we got her home she started literally pushing us around. Grace's signature move is what we call "the push". It's like leaning but she uses it as a management style. There's nothing funnier than watching a five pound dog try to push over a sixty pound dog. Although we could ignore the push when she was a puppy, now Grace weighs sixty pounds too. Once you've been pushed, you stay pushed. Grace doesn't like to hear a lot of back talk. She'll be more than happy to push you again if you need it.

My purpose in writing this book is to relate all the good, fun, and interesting things I've learned by watching Weimaraners. It's not to get you to buy a Weimaraner. This breed has gone down the path of out of control popularity before and it didn't turn out well for the dogs. Weimaraner's take a good picture but they don't sit still for very long.

If you don't already know what owning a Weimaraner entails then don't get one. If you don't know that you can handle a high energy hunting dog then you probably can't. Not many people make the transition after the Weimaraner is purchased. These dogs are demanding, manipulative, sneaky, need constant walks, steal the covers, surf your counters, put nose marks on your windows, cut the cheese all the time, and generally get into everything. But, they are cute enough to make you think you can handle all that.

My Weimaraner conversion was a special case. Most people don't choose to change their life so drastically and unexpectedly. Most people won't give up all their free time to get pushed around by a Weimaraner. I had the great advantage of having a wife that knew what we were getting with a Weimaraner. Still, she would admit that we devote a ridiculous amount of time to our dogs. As much fun as it's been, it's not hard to imagine how it could have gone wrong.

I could have written this book in half the time if I didn't have to throw the ball for Sadie every thirty seconds and if Grace wasn't always trying to push me out of my chair. But I love having them around and I can't wait to see what we get into next.

Sadie

Mary Ann always said that she would get a Weimaraner at some point. So, it's not as if I didn't have some warning. We didn't have the room or the time for a dog right up until Mary Ann decided that we did. We are both "dog people" so it was inevitable that we'd eventually have a dog. But, we always ended the dog talk with the word "someday".

Someday seemed years in the future so I didn't worry about it too much. We both agreed that the time wasn't right. Life was too hectic to handle a dog that I had heard could be "chaotic". Then one day Mary Ann declared our Weimaraner window was open and someday was here. She said dog people need to have a dog. I proposed that we get a nice picture of a dog. Maybe even a dog calendar so we would have a new one every month. But no, she wanted a real one.

A Weimaraner puppy was available from a nearby friend of a friend at the bargain price of I don't want to know. And I still don't want to know how much we paid for Sadie. I've seen the price tags on Weimaraner's and other hunting dogs and they are insane. When I was growing up we got dogs at the dog pound. If you paid for the rabies shot, it was yours. Seeing these sky high prices always makes me think of some old timers I knew who thought it was crazy to pay any money at all for a dog. I don't want to know how much Sadie cost just in case I run into one of these guys. I can't tell what I don't know.

Buying Sadie was a smooth process because I had nothing to do with it. In fact, every process goes smoother the less I have to do with it. Mary Ann showed me a picture of a bunch of gray potatoes wearing different colored collars, pointed to one and said "That one's ours".

I was completely unaware to what extent my life was changing the day we picked up Sadie. Despite all the warnings, I still somehow thought we were getting a normal dog. No one told me what was going to happen. At least, no one told me enough times that I understood. I should have been more thoroughly warned.

Standing guard over Sadie's family was her father. He was a huge dog that put both paws on my shoulders and looked me straight in the eye. It gave me the impression he was making sure I was sturdy enough to take care of one of his pups, but he was probably trying to drive me into the ground. And it felt like he could do it. This is when the light bulb finally flickered on in my head and I realized that the dog that had me pinned to the wall was the grownup version of the one we were taking home. I remember thinking, "Wait a minute, how big does this dog get? This is what we are buying?" And "Where are we going to put a dog this big?"

Fortunately the females of the species are slightly smaller (usually) and Sadie is nowhere near as big as her dad. The whole pick up process took about ten minutes to my uninvolved eyes and we headed home as official Weimaraner "owners".

I rode in the back seat of the car with Sadie on the way home. We thought she'd be frightened or anxious about the movement of the car or being away from her litter mates for the first time. Maybe being around some strangers would bother her. Or maybe she'd be nervous about a new experience. I was there to reassure her with a soothing word and a pat on the head if she needed it. It's obvious now that if being around strangers bothered her, I wasn't going to be much help. After about two minutes I judged her state of mind to be "asleep" and then "snoring". Although we wouldn't learn this until Grace came along, Sadie is not what you would call an alpha dog. In fact she's more of an omega dog. She's quite ok with being last. I realize now that being around a whole litter of Weimaraner's probably wore her out and she was happy to leave.

I thought I knew what Mary Ann meant by "major time commitment", but I didn't. I thought it meant that I'd do the normal things that you do when you have a dog, like go on poop patrol everyday and keep the water bowl full. As I said, I've had dogs before, I know they come with responsibilities.

And I was somewhat ready to do my share.

Even though I'm a dog person, I was enjoying that time between dogs. The time when you appreciate not having to rush home to let the dog out. It's rare that I find myself with less to do on a daily basis and I was enjoying it. I missed my old dog but I didn't miss being a dog owner yet. Inevitably, I would have started looking for another dog, eventually, someday.

Little did I realize how far off I was in my estimate of the time Sadie would require. Rarely have I missed an estimate this badly. We wouldn't have to "make an adjustment" or "carve out some time" for a Weimaraner. She demanded a major restructuring of our lives. Mary Ann was committed to doing this right. If we weren't going to do it right, then why do it? The feeling was that the more effort we put into Sadie, the more we'd get out of her. I wasn't sure this was true because I'd never gotten that much out of a dog before. But I was all in, I didn't want to look back and say I should have tried harder.

Weimaraner's don't really come to live with you. They don't move in and have a small bed over in the corner where they sit and pose for you to admire. Don't kid yourself into thinking you can give the new Weimaraner a short tour of the place and, pointing to the small bed say, "This is where you'll be sleeping." You don't buy a few dog toys for the

Weimaraner to occupy it's time. They have their eye on everything you own the first minute they walk in the door. When you get a Weimaraner, you might as well sign over all your stuff to them. You will fight this at first. The very notion that your stuff is no longer your own will cause you to protest in a huff. "Not my stuff, we'll have discipline in my house." You will be happier when you get over this. You and the dog can come to some agreements later, just try not to get too attached to material things.

Like most successful sneak attacks, Sadie's takeover was complete before I knew it was happening. The first months were filled with playing around and getting to know each other. Mary Ann's mom and sister pitched in to keep Sadie occupied and out of trouble. What I didn't know was that while we were getting to know Sadie, she got to know us too. She did her due diligence in assessing the weaknesses in our defenses and how best to take the reins of power. Dogs watch their family very closely. It's how they learn what's going on in the house. Sadie decided that you catch more bees with honey and became everyone's buddy. Everyone in the family feels a strong connection to Sadie. Everyone thinks they are secretly Sadie's favorite. She sized us up and wrapped us around what passes for her little finger.

And then she took control of all household operations. No matter what you are doing, any task big or small, your chief Weimaraner in charge will be there with questions and suggestions about how you could do it better. Many times her suggested course of action is a return to bed. Some extra sleep might be needed if we hunt birds later. Things like vacuuming or trying to start the lawnmower are made more "interesting" with a Weimaraner trying to crawl into your lap. This is Sadie's way of telling you that her sleep time has been insufficient. If getting into your lap isn't feasible she'll just stomp her foot until you realize that what you are doing is not what her highness wants to do.

Although I've never seen her fold a single shirt, Sadie loves laundry day. Clean clothes right out of the dryer are kind of warm and smell good. That's not the kind of pile she usually likes to roll in but she makes an exception for laundry. If you turn your back on a pile of clothes you will soon find her sprawled out in them. It gives me motivation to fold them right away. Unfortunately, Sadie is only too happy to unfold the clothes and get them back in a nap configuration.

When Sadie first moved in, I spent my mornings doing school work. Sadie spent her mornings trying to get me to stop staring at books, computer screens, and keyboards. She doesn't value education at all. School work is the very last thing Sadie ever wants anyone to do because it usually involves sitting still. In fact, she's spent her entire life trying to get me to stop working and get out into the field.

Not only was sitting still a problem for Sadie, the simple act of taking a walk was no picnic. A nice walk is a highlight of any dog's day. They like to get out and smell what's going on in the neighborhood. But, the leash is not a natural ally of the Weimaraner. Sadie tolerated the leash for ten feet or so and then she got offended by it. I let Mary Ann handle Sadie's leash training. For a while it looked like Mary Ann was walking a tasmanian devil. This is where we first learned of the importance of "off the leash" time. We thought the dog park would be great. She could be off the leash and mingle with other dogs. This didn't go so well as she is not a big fan of the butt sniffing ritual. Her little tail was clamped shut. Sadie was more interested in mingling with the other dog owner's. It took her two minutes to give up the dog pack and start working the crowd. While the dog pack roamed through the park, Sadie was the lone dog surrounded by the dog people. They were scratching her ears and telling her what a good girl she was. Sadie never gets tired of hearing how beautiful she is. So, she does like the dog park, but she can do without the dogs.

Dinner time is a special event for Sadie. Not her dinner time, our dinner time. At dinner Sadie likes to work the table. Her basic strategy is to sit under the table and go lap to lap. She knows where her bread is buttered. I was told that feeding the dog at the table would start bad habits, so I don't do it. I don't keep track of how often she scores, no one announces that they have broken the "don't feed Sadie under the table" rule. But I know she wouldn't keep doing it if it wasn't profitable. She's a capitalist in that way. I know that during every meal, at some point, she'll be under the table with a paw on my foot or her head against my leg. This is just in case I have some food I'm looking to get rid of. I don't get the majority of her attention; she seems to stop by just to remind me that hey, she's here if I don't feel like cleaning that plate. These days Sadie has to compete with Grace for table time. But, they divide and conquer effectively. Sadie still generally stays under the table while Grace gives everyone an individualized push.

It's clear to me now that Sadie never cared whether I finished school or not. If she did then she wouldn't have begged me to play ball every time I sat down at the computer. She seems to think this is where I sit when I want to throw the ball to her. I am embarrassed to say that I turned assignments in late because I got caught up playing with Sadie and a simple game of toss the ball in the house escalated into throw the frisbee in the cornfield. After about fifty throws, I get tired of throwing the ball and she gives me what I call the "one more time" look. After another fifty throws the look doesn't work anymore and she takes a different approach. She will put the ball down on the chair next to me and pretend to look away. When I make a move toward the ball, she snatches it up and runs away with it. Then she prances around doing the "Ken's a sucker" dance. Then it all starts again. And it goes on for days, months, and years. Sadie has an endless array of tricks to make me think I can get the ball from her. Sometimes the ball hangs loosely from one tooth, just dangling there and nearly forgotten. Other times it sits precariously on the edge of the chair with only one toenail to keep it from falling to the ground. She goes to any length to show me that I can easily get the ball from her. "Go ahead Ken, try it."

Sadie's second favorite toy is a round piece of fabric with a rope sewed onto it that flies kind of like a frisbee. I threw this thing so many times in one day that I strained something in the throwing mechanisms of my arm or shoulder, or both. This injury prevented me from entertaining Sadie in the manner which she had become accustomed, for several months. I can throw the ball with either arm, but due to having broken my left arm too many times, I can only throw a frisbee with my right arm. I'd like to say that Sadie was patient with me while I healed up, but I think she lobbied to have me replaced.

As you might guess, there are moments of drama, as when I lose something I had been attached to. Sadie, or perhaps Grace, chewed my favorite hat to pieces. This hat was targeted in a deliberate attack. Both suspects had seen me wear the hat in question. And both had easy access to the hat. I just had to determine which Weimaraner had committed this act. During questioning, Sadie hung her head and acted generally remorseful. Grace looked at me as if to say, "Looks like someone chewed the hell out of your hat Ken." So, I felt that I knew which one was guilty. I accepted Sadie's apology and we all went online to get a new hat.

One night my sister in law's car broke down around midnight. She was parked in the church parking lot and I went to pick her up. It might seem unusual for someone to be at church at midnight but there's a perpetual adoration that runs twenty four hours a day. I've covered those late night and early morning hours myself.

I took Sadie with me as backup. We were headed to a church parking lot so I felt reasonably safe. Still, we would be in a city in the middle of the night. Sadie felt better coming along to personally make sure everything went smoothly.

I got to the church and left Sadie in the truck with all the windows down. I parked where she could see us and supervise the tow truck driver. A major operation like this requires one, maybe two, Weimaraner chiefs to pull off. We were watching the guy put the car on the tow truck when I saw a Weimaraner running around the empty parking lot. I must have been sleepy because my first thought was, "What are the chances that a wild Weimaraner would be running around the church this late at night?" Of course, it was Sadie, patrolling the perimeter and keeping us safe. She had jumped out the window of the truck to get a better view of the proceedings. I didn't get to see this dismount and I'm glad. It's not a short hop out the window of a full size truck.

I learned an important lesson that night. If a Weimaraner wants to get somewhere, they will do anything to get there. There might be a cursory assessment of the danger of such an action, Sadie probably looked at the ground for a second, but her desire to be in a different place quickly over ruled her common sense. And even though I know this about Weimaraner's now, I haven't always been able to remember it. Grace once jumped through the screen door rather than wait five seconds for me to open it. I had loaded the truck with some of her favorite hunting gear and I was going back to get her. I guess I was too slow and she wasn't taking any chances about not going along. My fault for not making it clear to her that we were taking her with us that day.

When I say that Weimaraner's turned my life upside down, I mean exactly that. Life with Sadie drastically changed things around the house. She has an endless energy for monopolizing everyone's time. Nothing is how it had been. If it isn't hunting season, mornings start when Sadie is ready for her first trip to the yard. Then she checks the kitchen counters for stray food. Then there's a quick drive to the farm so she can stretch her legs and get the latest smells. Back home again, Sadie will either take a nap on the couch or return to bed for more thorough sleeping. This is followed by running up and down the steps fifty or so times. Then, depending on her schedule, there's four or five hours of ball playing. In the early afternoon she suns herself on the back deck. In the hottest part of the summer she makes frequent trips inside to cool off and check to see if I'm still staring at the computer. The day is interspersed with periods of going berserk if any of the neighbors dare to show themselves. In the evening it's back to the farm for a rigorous work out. I don't mean we put Sadie through a rigorous workout. She has fields to explore and woods to investigate and she requires an escort to carry her water.

In addition to running her monarchy at home, Sadie maintains a policy of total immersion in our life while we're away from home. You could call it brainwashing, or you could say I've been conditioned. Either way, I'm a changed man. For a while I resisted this change because it seemed like I wasn't in control. Then, I began to think this entire life overhaul was my own idea. That helped me accept it all. There's no doubt that Sadie was glad that I was finally getting with the program.

I know it's some sort of mind control trick, but Sadie was

beginning to make me realize that my time at home was a lot more fun and rewarding than when I was away. It wasn't long before I was resenting the time I had to be at work and thinking of ways to maximize my time at home. Sadie had lots of suggestions.

I began to get messages from Sadie's stomach. On my way home from work, I could stop and pick up some treats. What a great surprise that would be for her. I caught myself the first time I made a detour for her on my way home. I asked myself what was happening here? There are plenty of treats at home, we don't need more. But, Sadie gets bored with them. What? Wait a minute. Let's assess the spell this dog has cast upon you Ken. It's easy to want to spoil a dog that seems so appreciative. But, it always causes problems later. If you tell a dog yes fifty times in a row, the first time you tell it no will be a problem. I had to fight the urge to surprise Sadie with new toys and treats whenever I came home. And I thought we were all doing well in that area until I saw presents under the Christmas tree with Sadie's name on them.

I wouldn't call our life in the P.S. (Pre-Sadie) era dull or humdrum. In those carefree days we travelled quite a bit. We flew all over the country to do whatever we wanted. There was, relatively, very little planning to do. When Sadie took over, we didn't do less traveling, we did less flying. Hunting began to take up a large chunk of our time. Dogs add a layer of complications to even a short hunting trip. It's hard enough to plan things without a Weimaraner running around yelling, "Prepare my camper!"

Sadie had to implement her boot-camp like Weimaraner program in order to whip us into the kind of shape she needed. It took some time because I'm a slow learner and my attention span is short. As you'll see, I had a long way to go to be able to enjoy the hunting aspect of a Weimaraner. But, eventually I became a willing member of her staff. We settled into a comfortable existence and everybody's happy.

It's amazing how much effort Mary Ann put into forcing me to have a Weimaraner. That's how I like to phrase it, but it was always a mutual effort. It's easy to see that Mary Ann and I embraced the changes that Sadie brought to our lives. We actually were ready for a Weimaraner. Of course some of the changes were easier than others. When I'm prying a frozen dog turd off the ground in the middle of January I have to remind myself of the upside. But, when I go back inside and see her little tail wagging at me it all seems worth it. That's truly amazing to me.

The great success that we enjoyed with Sadie made getting a second Weimaraner an easy decision. It had taken some effort, but I made the transition from the dog free life to happily living under a benevolent Weimaraner ruler.

Grace

With Sadie firmly established in the family and well on her way to being a prized hunting dog, we dared to think about a second Weimaraner. I had very little to do with the planning stages of Sadie's arrival. I had different goals this time. My two years on the other end of Sadie's leash qualified me as a near Weimaraner expert. I was going to be engaged and indispensable throughout the entire dog buying process.

However, it takes a long time to plan and make a Weimaraner and at some point I forgot all about it. I believe I had stopped receiving regular updates and put the whole matter out of my mind. This is a pattern with me.

At this time there was a lot of planning and research going on to find the right breeder and that was better left up to Mary Ann. All breeders looked alike to me because I had been thinking that buying a dog is like buying a car. You want to buy from a reputable dealer, but you don't need to know that much about them. I brought insightful questions to the table like, "Do they have Weimaraner's?" and "Can we see a display model?" Or, even better, "Can we get one that doesn't fart so much?"

While I was concerned with these crucial questions, Mary Ann was talking to and emailing potential breeders to find out what kind of people they were. Now seems like a good time to admit that I have no idea how Mary Ann found Grace's breeder.

The "right" kind of breeder was one that had the traditional hunting abilities of the Weimaraner as their first priority. These breeders are more concerned with the success of the breed than they are with making money. So, they are actually concerned with getting the right buyers. If you are breeding hunting dog's, and you care about the well being of your dogs, you aren't going to sell your dogs to people that don't hunt. With both parties being so picky I figured this wouldn't be resolved easily or quickly. But, it was. Mary Ann found a breeder that echoed all her concerns and the deal was made relatively quickly and completely behind my back.

While the deal to acquire Grace had gone through, I was steadily researching the business of dog breeding. I had recently learned that there were unscrupulous dog breeders in business strictly for the money. Imagine my shock when dog breeding turned out to be like everything else in the world. Actually, I was more surprised that there were any breeders that didn't do it all for the money. There are more of them than you would think and finding them is worth the extra work. You can't just do an Internet search for "the right breeder", it takes phone calls, emails, and effort.

Without knowing it I was about to blunder into another

hot debate. This one was about the value and even the morality of pure bred dogs. It seems that there is a point of view that says you shouldn't breed dogs as long as there are dogs to be rescued from shelters. That sounds ok, it makes it seem like this mindset has its priorities in order. However, there will always be dogs in shelters. It's a struggle that will always be with us. The real issue is irresponsible breeding of dogs. This is what needs to stop.

The reality is that responsible breeders do the job of the rescue shelter by working hard to get all their dogs into good homes. In fact they are able to place a high percentage of their dogs into very good homes. We have always said that we rescued Sadie and Grace. They both needed good homes as much as any other dog. The argument against pure breeding of dogs doesn't really work for me. If it's done the right way, it doesn't matter what kind of dog is being bred. We should all be trying to achieve the goal of every dog having a good home. There's no doubt about that being an admirable, if ultimately unreachable goal.

We felt fortunate with Sadie as she seems to have been bred with the couch in mind. But she still has a lot of desire to be in the field and can find birds with no problem. We've heard stories about dog owner's that can't say that. Sadie can hunt but it seems like we got lucky.

This new dog was going to be different. It was going to

have hunting lines on both sides and be absolutely crazy for birds. And smart? It was going to be the kind of dog that people say is "too smart for its own good". We were going to have to put safety locks on the cabinets. We were going to have to speak in code so the dog wouldn't know what we were saying. To say we had high hopes is an understatement.

We weren't looking for a carbon copy of Sadie, although that would have been okay. Grace exceeded our expectations in the brains department and she would scoff at the notion that she's a copy of any dog. However, she is not a dog that's "too smart for her own good" because she listens well. This keeps her from getting into too much trouble. This must have something to do with her bond with Mary Ann. For Grace, no one else really exists when Mary Ann is around. She studies Mary Ann intently. So, it's not surprising that she receives messages clearly. Grace looks at me as just another face in the pack. And still I don't have to tell her things twice. But, don't get the idea she thinks I'm ever in charge. Her attitude is more along the lines of, "Yeah yeah, I got it." than that of an obedient hunting dog. Sometimes I think she's sizing me up for a takeover.

With Grace I was exposed to another debate that rages about hunting dogs and show dogs. Does a dog have to be one or the other? Can it be both? Of course it can, the dog doesn't care, it's up to the owner. Weimaraner owner's are probably more sensitive to the show question because irresponsible breeding in the 1950's tended to emphasize show skills over hunting skills. And the breed lost something that took a long time to get back.

We had some sort of chance to show Grace. Not at any high level, but she is a good looking dog that could have had some success if the competition wasn't too tough. But, then she got too tall for the standard. Now she'd start with a serious fault because her height is over the allowable size for a female. We didn't know she'd develop into such a massive beast. But, it's ok because now that she is disqualified from dog shows, I can stop thinking about it. This is also perfectly fine with Mary Ann because she was looking for an excuse to get out of going to dog shows. It's all about hunting for Mary Ann.

So, dog shows were off the radar and Grace was settling in and pushing everyone around. And it wasn't long before she started attacking me daily. It wasn't unexpected because Sadie had done a similar thing.

When Sadie was a puppy we noticed she had this little nibble maneuver where she quickly grazes across the surface of something with quick little bites. It isn't really nibbling and it isn't exactly chewing either. Mary Ann dubbed it chibbling. It's a very efficient way of scratching an itch but she uses it other ways as well. It's like she's taking a sample of something, to see if it might be a treat.

Once in a while she'll chibble across my forearm, just to make sure I'm not smuggling treats. It's an odd sensation and seems like she could take the hair right off my arm without breaking the skin if she wanted to. She's refined the chibble. But, she wasn't always so good at it. I have a small scar from a particularly rough chibble back in the early years.

I've seen other dogs do this but not quite the way Sadie does it. And we always thought it was a trait that was exclusively hers. So we were surprised when Grace was chibbling the day she came home. She's a champion chibbler that has taken the art to new heights. This dog could chibble the siding right off your house. She could part the carpet like the Red Sea if you gave her time. And she's not cutting me any breaks either. The first time she ran across my arm with her chibbling I thought I'd been attacked with a can opener. Chibbling may be an instinct but it still takes practice to acquire a smooth style. After many months of chibbling walls, car seats, floors, furniture, me, dog beds, camper doors, pigeon houses, sidewalks, Sadie, driveways, corn fields, toilet paper rolls, seat belts, fifty dog toys, our deck, our bed, a half dozen books, and the tailgate of my truck, Grace can adjust her chibbler to any material, any job. She goes from course to fine and anywhere in between. That's why we call her Chibble Nation. Or, at least I called her Chibble Nation. Everyone else thought it was a dumb nickname. One thing's for sure though. When the Chibbler strikes you will know it.

Grace's takeover of the family was complicated by the presence of Sadie, for a minute. She ambitiously launched operation "Push" very early in her life. I suppose she didn't feel like she could wait. Our house had too much ball playing going on and not enough hunting. Grace's golden rule says that if you aren't hunting birds, you need to be getting ready to go hunting birds.

That is why she spends so much time watching the bird feeder. It hangs off a tall hook on our back deck. Grace spends some time each morning staring out the glass door at all the neighborhood birds that come visit. I'm sure she thinks the feeder is a great idea as a bait pile, it lures the birds right to us. Except, we never eat any of those birds, which is against her policy. Grace would never feed birds unless we are fattening them up for our lunch. I'm sure she wonders if we'll ever do the right thing and thin out the flocks of fat birds around here. Her vigil at the door reminds me daily that she has hunting on her mind.

Most mornings we spend some time over at Mary Ann's family farm. Grace likes to harass the crows in the corn fields. When she trots back to us after scaring a bunch of crows into the air she's as close to laughing as I've ever seen a dog.

There are a lot of things to occupy a dog at the farm. In

the summer, the old cherry trees drop fruit on the driveway and the sun bakes them on. Grace spends some time chibbling the dried cherries off the asphalt. It takes a little lower jaw action to get them loose. This is a modified chibble maneuver, only for the advanced dogs. I'm sure it's a delicious snack, but it makes me cringe like fingernails on a chalkboard.

When Grace decides to apply the modified chibble, no project is too large. One day she decided we needed a new deck and began deconstructing the old one. She started chibbling the deck and had made a big trench in it before we had to halt the operation and remind her that a new deck wasn't in the budget. She said, "Budget shmudget, I'm taking this thing down".

Needless to say, lots of things would be different if Grace was in charge. For one thing, we wouldn't spend time doing things that aren't hunting for birds. Grace doesn't approve of the whole hunting season concept. To her that means there are times that you can't hunt birds. And that kind of pro-bird policy is nonsense. I tried to explain to her that hunting seasons are a way of managing the bird populations so there will always be birds to hunt. This logic didn't impress her. Her idea of a hunting season is where we hunt a particular species until it is endangered and then give it five minutes to recover.

For a dog that likes to be in the field so much, she sure likes air conditioning. Grace would like to have her own personal air conditioning vent that never turns off. You will often find her sitting in front of a vent letting the cool air blow on her. When the air turns off she looks into the vent, disappointed. She's an a.c. hog in the truck too. Since she can't ride in the front, she hangs her head over the seat to get as close to the vent as possible. She constantly moves from one side to the other to see which vent has the coolest air. All of the vents are pointed right at her but she hops around so she maximizes her air. I tell her that she's working up a sweat trying to stay cool but I might as well tell her to stop breathing for all she listens. The first time she laid her head on my shoulder I thought it was because she likes me, but she was trying to steal my air. Now she puts her head on my shoulder to say, "I need more air". I give her unacceptable answers like, "It's already on high." She wants to install a better air conditioner that can always go up one more notch.

Grace lives in fear that she will miss something. Whatever it is going on, she wants her nose in the middle of it. Unlike Sadie, Grace needs to be in charge. Recent projects she and I have completed are planting tomatoes, installing a ceiling fan, and spreading mulch in the yard. She's a little bit bossy. On trash day she says, "Hey, where are you going with that trash? Let me smell that one more time." And she has a gruff management style with comments like, "You're doing it all wrong." and "Thumbs are wasted on you."

Of course, we've also written a book. I write early in the morning and Grace is the only one that generally gets up when I do. There's no sneaking out of bed with her. She's an early riser but that doesn't mean she won't go back to bed after a trip to the yard and giving me some instructions and a sleepy push. I often question my decision to write this book on a device with a touch screen. I wrote the entire book on an iPad. Grace likes it because it allows her to make corrections with her nose. But, I secretly go back and fix things. I never promised her editorial control.

This same obsession with control causes Grace to fight sleep. She can't take the chance that something might happen while she's out. Her head and eyelids have to get so very heavy that finally she literally drops off to sleep. Her ideal place to sleep is where she can keep a paw on each of us and an half opened eye on Sadie. That way no one can get up and leave the room without her knowing about it. I have to give her credit for her vigilance. A less committed dog would delegate more, but as she's said, "I don't have much to work with here."

With an unlimited security budget, I imagine she'd have cameras installed all over the house, inside and out, with banks of TV screens in her command center. A giant air conditioner would blow frosty air on her 24/7. From her central couch she'd be able to keep tabs on everyone in the house as well as anyone passing by outside. Remote control gun turrets would keep the air bird free. And water cannons would blow the squirrels right out of the yard, just for fun. With the proper funding, Grace could make our house the safest place imaginable.

This obsession with home security is the reason she only blinks about twice a day. She seems to think a lot can happen during the average blink. So, generally she doesn't do it. I once saw her win a staring contest with a statue. I've seen her stare at an airplane until it was out of sight, never blinking once.

Grace's brashness allows her to escape discipline. She'll walk into the middle of the living room with five people sitting around talking and go up to her ears in someone's purse. It only takes a word to get her to take her nose out. It's this quick response that keeps things from escalating into anything resembling real discipline. She just shrugs as if to say, "I thought I smelled peanut butter in there."

Grace the ingenue doesn't acknowledge that some things around the house are off limits, it would never occur to her. She just assumes that everything in the house was brought in for her. And she'd never think to try and hide something from us. Why would you hide something that is yours? We know Sadie is getting into trouble when we can't find her. Grace doesn't get into trouble because we can always find her. She comes barging into the room with a "Look what I found." attitude.

Grace has a weakness for paper. I don't see why it fascinates her so. It's like she thinks the picture on a box of crackers means the box is made of crackers. A lot of the time I think she is just trying to help out. We have a box where we put paper recycling. It's not unusual to drop a box or a piece of paper in there and turn around to see Grace with it in her mouth, like she's got to follow us around to keep the house from getting messed up. Sometimes women will leave their purses where Grace can get at them. These purses are full of paper and Grace knows where the special paper is hidden. I've seen her get a twenty dollar bill out of one and bring it to me. What a good dog! At least she's trying to contribute around here.

One of her favorite varieties is toilet paper. It's always looked like a nice snack on a rotisserie to Grace. Putting the paper on the dispenser hasn't happened in this house since Grace was tall enough to reach it. She used to unroll it onto the floor but that was apparently too much work so she started chibbling it right off the roll. Every so often she'll casually walk into the room with an entire roll hanging out the side of her mouth. Sometimes she'll mumble "Morning" on her way by, like a grumpy old man on his way to the bathroom. And other times she doesn't acknowledge that we're there at all. Then she'll flop down on her bed to chew it to pieces at her leisure. When you take it from her she never puts up a fight, it's like she didn't want it anyway. But you know she's thinking, "Really? How is what your going to do with it so much better than what I was going to do with it?"

We're always looking for ways to make things easier around here. And the dog industry is diligently working to make things for us to buy. The latest labor saving gadget we've acquired is an automatic doggie watering nipple. This is a thingie that attaches to a hose connection. Turn the water on and let it go. The dogs can get a cool drink whenever they want. The water drips quicker depending on how far you open the valve. And dogs love a drippy faucet. Grace is all over this thing. She's all about self service and she's already worked out the best way to get the water out. She hooks the nipple with a canine tooth and lets it flow. Grace likes the valve all the way open but this is a bad idea because she tries to drink all the water. I've told her there's plenty of water in there and she can save some for later but she doesn't believe me.

The first few days Sadie thought Grace had to turn the water on for her. But, after a few instructional demonstrations, Sadie has the hang of it too. The point of having this is so the dogs can get a drink without having to wait for us to remember they are thirsty. But, the flow is low enough that they can't really gulp a bunch of water right after running. So, this thing is a big hit, the only question is how well will it hold up. Someone turned the water off, (probably me) and Grace was seen giving it a forearm slap. Then she gave me the "This thing is broke already." look.

I've said before that I'm amazed at how happy Sadie and Grace are to see us when we walk in the door. Grace's version of the Weimaraner greeting includes bringing a shoe to the new arrival. I don't know if the shoe is supposed to be a gift or if she wants me to put it on. I suspect it has something to do with birds. A shoe is the closest thing to a bird she can find in the house so it's probably meant as a reminder, "Hey, remember me? The bird dog? Hint, hint."

The mob scene I face when I get home contains a level of unbridled joy that I'd like to feel on a regular basis. Many times I've fought my way in the door and waded through a Weimaraner wagfest that's like being mugged. I try to observe it objectively sometimes while still doing all I can to increase their excitement to even higher levels by talking, scratching, attacking, petting, playing, singing, teasing, and tackling. My assessment is that these dogs are deliriously in love with me for about five minutes. Then they go back to see what Mary Ann is up to.

I've tried to explain this exuberant greeting style in hopes that I could recreate it in myself. But, it may not be possible. Dogs really don't know when or even if I'm coming back when I leave. They don't take for granted that they will ever see me again. That would explain the uncontrollable wagging but I doubt I can get myself to that state.

I've read some books written by dog scientists to try and get a more reasoned explanation of the Weimaraner greeting ritual. Reading these books is a little like talking to someone that makes movies. It takes a lot of the fun and mystery out of it when you know how the tricks work. These dog books sometimes tell you too much about what is really going on in your dog's head. A generically scientific response to the question of why Sadie and Grace are so insanely happy to see me when I get home would go something like this: "The dogs aren't happy to see you. That's a common mistake made by laymen. What you are observing is the familial paradigm being played out in conjunction with the dog's experience of success in getting food from you in the past. In addition, the juxtaposition of your response compared to others already in the house makes for a heightened communicative display and possibly relieves some of the dog's anxiety." Or something like that, I made it all up. I don't find the scientific explanations tremendously helpful. But, I still read the books just in case.

I've concluded that people have too much information to be as happy as dogs. It's a downside to being human and a consequence of living in an information age. I'd love to be less informed, especially if it would make me happier. Then again, if a dog's happiness is balanced by an equal sadness or anxiety, that's an emotional roller coaster I don't need to ride. I'll just continue to be greeted by these two knuckleheads and vicariously enjoy their happiness.

Two Weimaraner's have been better than one for us. It's double the fun without being double the trouble. The key is space, if you have enough space where you live, filling it with a Weimaraner is a good idea.

Grace fit into our family like a missing piece. We needed a take charge kind of dog to handle security and generally complement Sadie. The contrast of Grace's personality to Sadie's creates a dynamic around the house that's more interesting than if they had been just alike. The addition of Grace has been such a success that thoughts of another Weimaraner are only natural. But, the beds and couches are full. While two Weimaraner's are as easy to take care of as one, a third might tip the scales over.

Hunting

So now that we had a Weimaraner there were certain steps we were going to have to take to make this a successful enterprise. Mary Ann stressed the "hunting" in "hunting dog". That's what they were bred to do and that's what we were going to do. These dogs will only reach their true happiness potential if they get to hunt often.

Weimaraners are not for laying around the house taking up space on the sofa. Although, the exhausted Weimaraner excels at this after a day of hunting. So do the hunters. I never doubted that Sadie would see a lot of the field because Mary Ann has hunted for as long as I've known her. Deer, bear, fox, pheasants, geese, turkey, grouse, and assorted varmints are all on her list. She seemed to think hunting with a dog would be great fun. I thought it sounded dangerous and crazy. Sadie seemed up for anything.

Hunting is a big part of her life, but Mary Ann never put any pressure on me to become a hunter. Although, she's good at making me think things are my own idea, so I'm not sure that she wasn't using mind tricks on me.

I had never been hunting at that point. I couldn't honestly say I saw the attraction. I didn't know if I wanted to be a hunter and I had no idea if I could be good at it. I always figured that hunting was something you started at a young age or you didn't start it at all. Now I know that's not true, lots of people start hunting as adults. Robert Ruark called it the horn of the hunter. Some people hear it early and some hear it late. Some don't hear it at all and just go to the grocery store. I wasn't hearing the horn blow all that loudly yet, it was just at the edge of my hearing.

I knew that as soon as Sadie was ready, Mary Ann would have her out in the field hunting birds. This gave me some time but I didn't know how much and I wasn't counting on it being more than a year. I had no idea how long it took to train a hunting dog but I knew Mary Ann would fast track Sadie as much as possible. From the way she was describing it, this training was going to take up a lot of time and money. This was going to be time she didn't spend with me if I didn't hunt and that was clearly unacceptable. So, I decided to give hunting a try until such time that I loved it or completely hated it or was so bad at it that I was asked to stop hunting by the President of the National Hunting Association, or whatever group runs things. Turns out there is no president of the NHA, and there is no NHA either. Fortunately, hunters are a lot less organized than I imagined.

That's all there was to it. Just like that I was a hunter. My decision was made easier in that I was not against the idea of hunting from the beginning. In fact, I was very pro-hunting because I'm very pro-eating and I like guns. I had no ideological barriers to prevent me from being a hunter and I realize now that I was pretty lucky that was the case. People that are anti-hunting have a lot further to travel, ideologically, than I did. I started thinking of myself as a hunter right away, just to see how I liked it, despite the fact that I'd never actually done it.

To become a hunter for real, and not just in name, I gathered all the information I had about hunting. This didn't take long because everything I knew about hunting consisted of things Mary Ann had told me. It was obvious that I hadn't been paying much attention and was probably just hoping she didn't quiz me on it later.

We'd been watching hunting shows on TV for years so I figured some of that must have sunk in. But trying to say exactly what I had learned was more difficult. Those shows usually go something like this: pretty scenery, guy whispers something into the camera then shoots an animal. It's usually a perfect shot even if they don't find the animal until the next day. I didn't see many hunters miss on all the goose video's I watched. And I was pretty sure my shots weren't going to be as good. I had to admit that I hadn't learned anything useful from all those TV shows.

So let's see, I knew next to nothing about animals, guns, gear, or tactics. And I certainly didn't know enough about the many millions of federal and state laws that would affect my hunting experience.

Animals were a big subject but at least I was able to focus solely on birds since that was going to be my initial prey. Then I discovered how many different kinds of birds there are. At first, all the birds looked alike to me. I mean exactly alike. I couldn't tell a flock of geese from a flock of seagulls. I found that looking at pictures of birds in books is only somewhat helpful. When you only get a quick glimpse of a bird exploding out of cover it doesn't look like the picture. I found myself saying "Hold still so I can tell if I'm allowed to shoot you." all the time. The first time I saw a grouse, I didn't really see it. It disappeared in the trees so fast I only had a suspicion that it was a grouse. It could have been a flying squirrel for all I knew. Someone took a shot at it and confirmed that it was a grouse. But, they missed and I will always wonder about it. Bird identification is critical most of the time. When you are in a field or in woods that contains both legal and illegal birds you really don't want to shoot the wrong one. The fines quoted to me are steep and not in my budget.

Guns were another huge subject that I was anxious to tackle. I'll never know as much about guns as I'd like to because I want to know everything. I could dedicate my life to learning all there is to know about guns and still never accomplish it. There are just too many different kinds. And gun history, while fascinating, is elaborate and long. The more I learn about guns the more there is to know. It gets easier over time, especially because its so interesting, but at first it was filling my brain with too many details. It's important to keep things simple, at first. I wasn't going to be hunting cape buffalo so I reluctantly put those articles aside. I wasn't even going to be hunting deer. My area was much more specialized and that helped immensely. Since there are only a million or so guns you can shoot birds with, I figured to have a good handle on my options in about five years. Then I realized that since I only had one gun that would be the best place to focus my efforts. First get familiar with one gun and then worry about the rest. I had been starting a wish list when what I needed to do was go out and shoot my shotgun.

Beyond the generally obvious things like "be still" and "lead the bird" I wasn't aware that there were hunting tactics. But, its amazing how much work happens before the deer hunter gets to sit still or the bird hunter gets to shoot. I defined tactics as those things you do to get the animal to stand still long enough for you to shoot it. But, I was still thinking of deer hunting and TV shows. My definition had to change immediately because Sadie and I were after birds, so there wasn't going to be any standing still. I knew that you shoot them when they fly but how to get to that point was a mystery. I figured that tactics would be involved at some point.

Hunting is highly regulated so you have stay on top of things to keep from paying fines, going to jail, or getting your stuff confiscated. We like to keep things legal around here. Its usually very easy to get the government to tell you what you have to buy to engage in whatever activity you have in mind. Hunting is slightly different in that it's not easy to get all the information you may need. You can spend as much money as you want on licenses and stamps and stuff and still miss something. We were always discovering a new stamp we had to buy to hunt this animal over in that spot at this time of year. And still, I always think the DNR officer is going to say we overlooked a new special stamp and we're all under arrest. I needed to find out how hunter's kept up with all the laws.

On top of all these challenges I also had to learn why we needed Sadie. And I believe Sadie was wondering why we needed me. Clearly I needed to start reading and paying attention so I would be ready before Sadie was.

Of course, the first place I turned was the Internet. The Internet has plenty of information on hunting and Sadie doesn't use it. That would be my advantage. It's easy to jump right in and start reading so I did. I knew the Internet would bombard me with too much information and I'd end up sorting through a lot of ads before I got to anything interesting. And it did. Even though I was ready for information overload, the net quickly became overwhelming. There are magazines with free articles, lots of forums with people happy to answer your questions, more than a few angry people, umpteen associations, societies, and groups to join for a small fee, and more sites tailored to specific kinds of hunting than I would have believed possible. I was amazed at the number of ads for African safaris. I had no idea they still had African safaris. A safari seems way to cool to still exist. If there's one thing you would think our over regulated politically correct society would have outlawed by now it's safaris. I'm sure the Maryland Legislature would like to regulate African safaris if it could figure out how to do it. Riding around in an open vehicle all day shooting exotic animals and then drinking around the fire all night seems like an obvious target for the busybodies to stamp out. I suppose the reason is that safari's still exist is that they still benefit the African economies.

One source of information that I came to rely on was a radio show about hunting and fishing that comes on Saturday mornings from a station in Baltimore, of all places. It's essentially a one man show where the host talks about what's happening in the outdoorsman world. It had been on for years but was never on my radar. Now, it was as if the clouds parted and the show was sitting there with all the information

I needed. This show was all about solving mysteries for me. The dense cloud of hunting code talk got clearer every time I listened to this show. I didn't know anything, so in the beginning everything he said was useful. He went on about seasons, licenses, fees, regulations, legislators good and bad, deer, geese, ducks, fish, the DNR, and all kinds of other stuff. Even when I didn't know what he was talking about I could go ask Mary Ann. If the weather was good I could get this show on my truck radio all the way down into Montgomery County, the anti-hunting capital of the world. Or, at least the state. Listening to a hunting show while driving through Montgomery County feels like getting away with something. I credit this show with giving me a ton of great information but the best thing it did was make hunting real for me. I knew now that there were a lot of people getting up early and going out hunting. More than I had previously believed. But, the mainstream media in Maryland will tell you that there isn't much hunting going on in Maryland. They downplay the popularity of hunting because they don't like it. Progressives have even removed the hunting tab from the front page of the Maryland DNR website. It used to reside next to the fishing tab, but not anymore. The anti-hunting crowd don't like to admit how much many people love hunting in Maryland. Or how much money hunting adds to the Maryland economy.

By listening to this show, I learned when the different hunting seasons occurred. I learned what hunter's would be doing at certain times of the year, and where they would be doing it. After some time, I knew what the people would be talking about when they called in to the show. I knew when they would be fired up about some new law the legislature had dreamed up and what group was behind it. I also gained a new appreciation for the importance of the Chesapeake Bay.

The Chesapeake Bay runs right through Maryland. It almost cuts it in half. I've always preferred the eastern side. When I became a bird hunter that preference increased by a hundred. Although the far western part of Maryland is attractive to deer hunters, I wasn't interested in deer, yet.

It would be difficult to overstate the importance of the Chesapeake Bay to Maryland. It provides many people with their livelihood. There are commercial fishermen and crabbers sure, but there are thousands of other people who's jobs depend on the bay. Even more importantly, it provides Maryland with it's real identity. It's a state that is very focused on hunting and fishing. The competing identity which the state gets from Montgomery and Howard counties is not nearly as compelling. Their slogan of "We've got a boatload of lawyers." just doesn't convey the same sense of Maryland life.

That's why I wish that the eastern shore would secede

from the rest of Maryland and become its own state. I'd move there immediately if that happened. Unless the borders were already closed, in which case I'd apply for citizenship.

As expected, Mary Ann had Sadie out at training classes before too long. Sadie and Mary Ann went through some tough training in the months leading up to the opening of hunting season for upland game birds. When they got home from these classes they were totally worn out. I've never seen the two of them need a nap as much as they did then. They were both learning a lot, but most importantly they were developing the indispensable bond between a hunter and their dog.

Based on their level of exhaustion, I was willing to let Sadie and Mary Ann do all the field training they wanted without me. I knew there would be a place for me once the real hunting started. I concentrated on learning what I could about the art of bird hunting. And it wasn't long before we were out in the field to see what we could do with all our new knowledge.

Although I knew it was important to keep my eye on Sadie in the field because she would be the one finding the birds, I found it difficult. My scatterbrained thoughts that first morning went something like this. "Ok Ken, be safe and have fun. Keep your eye on Sadie. Is my safety on? It's kind of cool out here, I hope I wore enough clothes. Did I bring enough shells? Is one box enough? Wait, did I put shells in the gun? This ground is kind of muddy, hope I don't trip on these roots. How water resistant are these boots? Where did Sadie go? It's hard to hear with these ear plugs in. My foot is getting cold. Wonder if I should pick up the empty shells off the ground. I think my sock is getting wet. How did Sadie get way over there? Why is Mary Ann waving at me? Wow, those chuckar's are fast, how am I going to hit that? Why is Sadie looking at me like that? It's kind of warm out here. Why did I wear a long sleeve t-shirt?"

My mind was on everything but hunting. There were more things going on than I thought there would be. I blamed it on a.m. grogginess. Morning is not my best time of day and we had started the day early. Hunting is gear intensive, you need a lot of stuff. And you take a lot more stuff that you could do without but might somehow need. I tried to pack as much ahead of time as I could. I put everything I would need in a pile where I could find it in an early morning daze and still struggled to get it all. No doubt this was a test Mary Ann had planned for me and I was failing it with no problem. She had her gear, Sadie's gear, and some gear I had forgotten, like my gun. Although I've gotten much more organized, it's still a tradition that I lose my hunting license the night before we go hunting and forget at least one thing I need.

The biggest problem with being so scatter brained that

morning was that I, probably, negatively impacted the hunt, which was really a training session for Sadie. A number of times Sadie was on point and I was fifty yards away. This was just a bit too far for Sadie at that stage in her career. Either she broke in on those birds or Mary Ann didn't wait for me and shot them herself.

Somehow I did end up shooting a few birds that day. And Sadie did well, she found all the birds and her pointing showed progress. Mary Ann didn't give me a hard time about being distracted, slow, shooting bad, or giving Sadie bad cues. But, Sadie was not so nice. She was giving me exasperated and frustrated looks all day. She even snorted at me once. I know she was upset with me because we spend so much time together at home and at the farm. We do a lot of visual communicating. I can look at Sadie and tell her that Mary Ann is home and is about to open the door, without saying a word. She can look at me and tell me if she wants to go out, wants food, wants to play ball, or just wants my chair. She even has a special look if she can't find her ball. So, we make a lot of eye contact throughout the day and I could tell she wasn't happy with me.

Grace is the exact opposite. She rarely looks me in the eye. I believe she thinks that since she's already seen me once there's no reason to look at me again. Unless I have just walked in the door and she's in greeting mode, she's got better things to look at. There's more verbal communication with her. She stands by the door or gives a bark if she wants to go out. And I am invisible in the field to her. When I say something to her she acts surprised to see me. When we are hunting, Grace is focused on birds. She might make time to acknowledge Mary Ann but that's it. (Immediately after I wrote that I walked into the living room. Sadie was asleep on a pillow and Grace was on the couch next to her staring a hole right through me. I stared back as best I could to see if she would blink but she didn't.)

Sadie and I worked all our issues out. Our days in the field are much happier and smoother than that first time. Grace still doesn't pay much attention to me. When I shoot a bird she turns around as if to say, "Who shot that one? Oh, when did you get here Ken?"

Not surprisingly, Sadie's finest moment coincides with one of my worst. We were hunting a strip of land and were just about to quit for the day. Sadie made a sharp right turn out of the brush and headed across a cut down corn field, nose to the ground. Mary Ann and I watched her go, reluctant to follow after we'd hunted for four hours or so. Sadie was steadily making progress across a three hundred yard field and we were not about to humor her. I yelled to Sadie, "Hey crazy dog, there's no birds over there." My vote was to let her go, then wait for her to return in shame, hanging her head and tail. Sadie got across the field, took a step into the brush at the edge and went on point. And it was steady. Her back feet were still in the corn field. I was unimpressed. Mary Ann started trudging across the field. But, not me. I started giving reasons not to go. "There can't be a bird there", "If there is a bird there, it will run before we get there", "We already saw all the ones that were planted", "I'm tired of hunting", "Sadie won't hold a point that long", "The bag is already full". Nothing worked, Mary Ann was going to call Sadie's bluff.

I don't know how long it took for me to get across that field. I was walking slow, grumbling under my breath. I knew this would be pointless.

Finally, I was in position, shaking my head. Mary Ann went in to flush the bird. It broke away from me and she shot it.

Yes, I was surprised that Sadie tracked that bird from so far away and that she held point for close to ten minutes. And yes, I felt like a cement head for doubting the Weimaraner nose.

I learned something that day. Sadie tried to make me look bad in front of my wife on purpose. She's a sneaky dog and it's not a good idea to turn your back on her. I haven't yet found a way to repay her that is nearly good enough. The lesson I should have learned is to trust our dogs, but Sadie's misbehavior made that impossible.

Eating is a big part of hunting. That may seem obvious but what I mean is that hunting makes you appreciate eating more than you ever will with store bought food. I come from a long line of eaters, but not hunter's. So, looking at one of the first birds I ever shot and seeing the feathers, blood, and dog slobber on it, I wasn't thinking it looked like dinner. That's where Mary Ann comes in. Her extensive experience in preparing all manner of food in a variety of ways is awesome to behold. She cooks better on a campfire than most people do on a stove. So, I had an easy transition from looking at that first bird and saying "I'm not eating that." to being able to see the end product and knowing the steps to getting it there.

The process of getting the bird from the field to the plate is a fair amount of work but it holds hidden value. It makes you self sufficient. It gives you confidence that you could survive if you had to.

At least, I think I could survive. There have been enough post-apocalyptic movie's that this kind of survival is on a lot of people's minds. Everyone runs through doomsday scenarios to try to see what we would have to do if something happened to cause the breakdown of our society. I never get very far into it before I realize that there would be problems that I don't know how to solve. Finding fresh water on a long term basis is one of them. Shooting a few birds for dinner might be the easiest thing I have to do. Of course, I hope our society never collapses to the point that I have to go hunting to put food on the table. But, at least I won't be completely clueless if it does.

Aside from the doomsday sort of survival, there's the kind of survival that we can practice right now. You have to learn some basic skills but it isn't that difficult. Now that I have those skills I look forward to hunting because it's a chance to get better at it. It took a fair amount of work just to get to the point where it's fun. But, it was "fun" work.

After all this effort, I found that a lot of people don't appreciate hunting or hunters. When you mention that you go hunting, some people look at you with varying degrees of pity and disdain. One guy told me it wasn't very civilized. While he was eating a bowl of chili. I said it didn't make me feel good to have other people do my killing for me. I was lashing out, I admit it. I was trying to defend my new found hunter status and I probably went too far. But, it was clear that I was supposed to feel ashamed of being a hunter. And I hadn't even hunted very much or done it very well. I can only imagine the animosity that hunter's that have killed lions must face.

For some reason there are American's that don't think anyone should own guns. And if you do, it should only be something that is hidden in your closet to be broken out only when someone breaks into your house. I don't understand that attitude and never will. The other reaction is from "animal lover's" that don't think people should kill animals ever. Unless it's cows in a building far away from where anyone can see it and really we shouldn't eat so many hamburgers anyway. I can sympathize somewhat with this viewpoint since it was drilled into my head for so much of my life. We should always respect the animals we hunt and eat. At this point in history it's a privilege to still be able to hunt. We should not take it for granted.

I struggled with the actual act of killing animals when I began hunting. Then some things clicked into place for me that put things in perspective.

The first was that we are called to be good stewards of the environment and the animals God placed on the earth. That doesn't mean we don't kill them as we need to. It means we respect them and we never take lightly the fact that we are taking another beings life.

The second thing was a dvd I saw on animals dying of natural causes in the wild. If you think it's cruel to kill an animal with a shotgun then you haven't seen the way a deer dies of natural causes. Nature is both incredibly beautiful and unimaginably harsh.

The third thing that made killing animals ok for me was tasting goose. Geese are birds, I've seen them fly. That's where their similarity with other birds ends. I thought a goose tasted like a chicken, or maybe a duck. Wrong, it's totally different. It's more like beef. How this is possible I do not know. And I no longer care. A crockpot full of goose is one of those pleasures that make all the work worthwhile. I will be there every year taking all the geese I can get and if you want me to feel ashamed, forget it.

Sadie Loses A Nail

It was a Sunday. We'd been to the farm. We arrived home as usual after a nice walk. No one suspected that events were about to unfold that would disrupt our lives for weeks. Well, that might be overstating it somewhat, but I was definitely inconvenienced several times for weeks.

Just as she's done a thousand times before, Sadie jumped out of the truck. But, this time she hooked a toe nail on something and ripped it right off. I mean completely off. It came off clean as a cap off a pen.

Sadie let out a cry of pain that was different than we had ever heard. I now think she may have been faking all those other times. It was a single yelp, loud and sincere. After the yelp she was surprisingly calm. There was no follow up yelp or crying, whining, or complaining. We were frantic. I carried her into the house and got her onto a dog bed in the kitchen. Okay, that makes for a good image, but truthfully, Sadie walked in the house and plopped down on her bed. I carried Mary Ann into the house, screaming and crying about poor Sadie.

There was some blood, but it wasn't bad. My injury assessment skills have evolved over time. I used to classify an injury as "bad" if I saw any blood. But, we had so many of these that I adjusted the "bad" label to include only injuries that had "a lot" of blood. Now, I've arrived at the point where it has to be gushing before I declare it to be "bad".

This is the type of injury that is difficult to handle. It would previously have been considered "bad" due to the amount of blood on the floor. It clearly needed some kind of treatment and a bandage. Just as clearly was the fact that it was too painful to touch. Sadie wasn't going to let us do anything to it without a fight.

We weren't confident about how to proceed so we went immediately to the Internet. A reliable Internet connection is very helpful these days. Just don't get addicted to it. One day the Internet will shut off and you will find yourself a much less competent person than you were before the Internet ruined you.

We also have a comprehensive dog first aid book that is very helpful. It covers all the likely injuries and doesn't spare the gory details, including graphic pictures. There's no way to overestimate how important preparation is in an emergency like this. A strong stomach doesn't hurt either. We're able to test our stomach just by looking at the pictures in the first aid book. Some people get queasy at the sight of blood. I'm lucky in that it doesn't bother me. I've also seen a number of people that can hold things together long enough to do what needs to get done. But, they want to puke the whole time.

After some vet consultation and more Internet research we discovered that this was actually a minor injury but it needs to be taken care of quickly. Our first aid book has a good example of how to bandage a dog paw. As usual the first one was awkward but soon Mary Ann was an expert at it.

The hard part for Sadie is that she could not be allowed to lick her paw. That did not stop her from trying and we spent the next week in a non stop struggle to keep the bandage dry and unlicked. There were a few tough times. Both sides had some victories and some setbacks. Harsh words were spoken and quickly forgotten. At one point Sadie even wore the dreaded cone. But, we all got through the first week relatively unscathed. Mary Ann and I got to sharpen our first aid skills and we all learned a new word, cornification.

Everything we had read and heard said that after a week we should be able to take the bandage off. But, after two weeks the progress was slow.

Sadie had about fifteen different kinds of experimental bandages, shoes, socks, and bags on her paw by the end of two weeks. Then she was finally healed up enough to be out of the gauze and vet wrap combination that had become such a big part of our day. We came to realize that this injury was going to be a longer term project than we were led to believe. And Sadie wasn't at her best during this convalescence. She had a difference of opinion about the treatment of this injury from the beginning. We can only empathize with her and tell her we know the urge to lick it is probably overwhelming. I even told her the problem was that when the only tool you have is a tongue, everything starts to look like an ice cream cone. She gave me that "You just don't get it." look.

My favorite package of dog foot protector was multi-layered old sock, field shoe, and newspaper rain bag held on with some velcro. This combination was quite effective in protecting the paw from hazards such as dew, rain, rough terrain and Sadie's tongue.

This was the kind of injury that everyone was getting tired of dealing with after two weeks, especially Sadie. No one likes to be a patient for that long and she was beginning to hide when we got out the first aid kit.

Also she just wasn't able to run full speed in any of the myriad things we put on her foot to protect it. At first I thought it was just that we couldn't come up with anything that was both effective and comfortable. Most of the things we tried seemed awkward after fifteen minutes or so. But, a big part of it was that the nail was bothering her. She couldn't stop holding the paw in the air even a week after the incident.

It took much longer than it should have but the nail was finally cornified and Sadie's spirits returned normal. This episode was another good example of how labor intensive a dog can be when the inevitable injuries occur. Someone pointed out to me that many dogs that aren't as active as our Weimaraner's can go their whole life without this kind of injury. I guess that's true but if you choose a high energy dog eventually you will need a bunch of gauze pads and a few miles of vet wrap.

Hunt Tests

As with everything else about dogs and hunting, I had a lot to learn about hunt tests. Once again I waded into an age old debate that I didn't even know was raging around me.

What is the value of hunt tests? What are they for? What do they prove? Who do they benefit? The answer to all those questions is that we go to hunt tests because we want to. In his book "The Complete Weimaraner", William Denlinger puts it best when he says "The purpose of a hunting dog is to give pleasure to its owner." Denlinger wrote that in 1953. And most people today wouldn't phrase it that way. What he means is that we don't have to justify our hunt tests to people that don't like it or understand it. Dogs don't care about hunt tests, even though they seem to enjoy them. The owner's, breeders, and organizations participate in hunt tests because we still can. There's no reason to care what other people think about it.

There's also no reason to think that a dog needs a title to be a good hunter. The truth is that there are great hunting dogs that never went to a hunt test in their life. They were too busy hunting. Ok, so there's another debate settled.

I've never liked tests or quizzes in general because they are opportunities to show how much I don't know. The difference with hunt tests is that the dog doesn't necessarily know that they are being tested on this particular day in the field. Although I wouldn't be surprised if the dogs knew that something different was going on. There's not usually so many other dogs in the field with us, not to mention strangers on horses.

Our first hunt test was held near Gettysburg by the Weimaraner Club of Washington DC. The impossibility of having a hunt test inside the borders of D.C. is obvious. It's a place where city officials look at the second amendment as an inconvenience.

I had never seen so many Weimaraner's in one place before. It's unusual for me to see a Weimaraner in a car where we live. So the first few that rolled into the hunting grounds were a surprise to me. Hey, they've got Weimaraner's too! After the fifteenth car full of Weimaraner's went by, I started to feel foolish standing in the parking lot pointing at cars. I got the idea that there would be a lot of Weimaraner's in attendance that day. I'm quick on the pickup like that.

Wherever we go, Sadie and Grace are the only Weimaraner's around. It's easy to think that you've got some kind of rare dog. People come up to us and ask what kind of dog they are all the time. When we say "Weimaraner", they usually say "Weimawhatta?" or they just nod and say "Oh, that's what I thought."

Here at this test I was seeing so many people with Weimaraner's I was feeling a lot less special and rare. Some people had more Weimaraner's than me, a bigger pack, and I didn't like it. I quickly reigned that thought in. Two was our limit, at least for now, and I knew it. I wasn't going to start placing orders for new dogs just to compete.

I showed up unprepared as usual. I thought there would be an official list of rules handed out but there was nothing. That takes all the pressure off because no one gives you a real hard time when you break rules you didn't know about. They say ignorance is no excuse but unless you are in court, it is. Mary Ann had gotten all the rules and regulations off the web site anyway, so she was set. I asked her not to tell me any of them.

We told Sadie and Grace that this was a test. Which is probably cheating. But it didn't seem to spook them and nobody with a name tag asked about it so mum's the word on that. I was beginning to feel like one of those hockey parents, I wanted Sadie and Grace to have every advantage I could gain for them so they'd do well. Turns out I had very little to offer in terms of hunt test preparation. My main contribution was driving the truck.

From my perspective, Mary Ann took the dogs to the field and came back forty minutes later. Then they gave us some big orange ribbons, we took some pictures, and went back to our campsite.

The judges needed horses to keep up so an observer on foot like me didn't have much chance to see anything. Here's what happens, according to my agent in the field. This was a test for the junior hunter ribbon. Birds are planted in the fields, usually quail or chuckar, and the dogs are set loose to find and point them. The dogs are judged on how many birds they find, how well they hold their point, and how steady they are to the shot. There are a lot more details to the test but that is essentially it. It's surprising how many people, upon hearing that description, say "What happens to the birds?". As if the process can't be approved if something untoward happens to the birds. People can be surprisingly concerned for all animals except the ones that end up on their plate.

Mary Ann came back from the field unhappy both times. Both dogs easily passed the test but she was already looking for ways to improve. This is her standard reaction but she soon realizes that when all the stated goals have been met it's okay to celebrate a bit. The critique can wait until later.

I give my first hunt test experience an A-. I had a good time, met other people that try to own Weimaraner's, learned a lot, and had a good barbecue sandwich. More importantly, I now had a clear picture of where we were trying to get to with the dogs hunting skills. I would have liked to see more of the actual test but that was my fault for not being able to run as fast as a horse.

Our next hunt test was further away and so was a more elaborate trip. We drove four hours with the camper to a state park near Hazelton Pennsylvania. The circumstances would be a little different because we were testing at a German Shorthaired Pointer club. We didn't know if there would be other Weimaraner's there but didn't care. We figured dog people at a hunt test are pretty much the same no matter where you go. And that was generally true. We only encountered one guy that had the "It's a shame what they've done to the Weimaraner." attitude. But, he wasn't a judge and he was probably surprised when our dogs hunted better than the GSP he was handling.

I suppose we will always meet people that don't know that Weimaraner's have made a strong comeback as hunter's since the show dog days. That's ok, I don't mind telling people about it. Especially at hunt tests because we are in a position to show them, not just tell them. Although, maybe that guy just liked GSP's better than Weimaraner's.

The club house was the standard cinder block building, nothing special. But, they were cooking bacon, egg, and cheese sandwiches inside. The value of any event is greatly enhanced by a bacon, egg, and cheese sandwich.

Someone had staked out a pack of wild Viszla's in front of the club house. We had to walk this gauntlet to get from our truck to the sandwiches and back again. These were young Viszla's and they were barking their heads off at all the people. Viszla's are a little smaller than I had imagined but are great looking dogs.

Although the club house was standard, the grounds it sat on were beautiful. The land in the back of the house dropped off into a valley with every imaginable type of cover growing in it. It was October so the fall colors were out in force. The club had clearly gone out of their way to plant so many varieties of cover that the patchwork fields added to the beautiful contrasting colors. This vantage point gave a great view of the senior hunt test area right from the tables and benches behind the house. We were able to watch quite a few of these tests without getting too far from the grill. It was a valuable learning experience for me as I had never seen live tests like this. These tests weren't just a formality, the judges were tough. Less than half the dogs we watched got qualifying scores. There were no Weimaraner's in the senior hunt group though.

All the judges I met seemed to have enough experience to know that Weimaraner's are great hunting dogs. They just needed to see these particular dogs in action. I had been preparing myself for some kind of bias against our dogs because of things I'd heard and read. However, these judges had no preconceived notion that all the hunting instincts had been bred out of Weimaraner's. We weren't starting out having to prove that we belonged there. That's about all you can ask from a judge.

I got to see these tests in their entirety. Not because I was able to run any faster than before, the grounds were just more conducive to observers.

I knew there was nothing Sadie and Grace couldn't handle in these tests but I still got anxious as the time approached for the first brace. I was more nervous than either dog. My desire for them to be successful had been growing by the minute since we arrived at the test area. I was seeing how hunt tests could become so important to dog owners. The more I told myself it didn't matter, the more it actually did.

Sadie was first on the line. Her brace mate was a GSP. They blew the whistle and she was off. I was wondering how the dogs would affect each other. I've seen Sadie get distracted by other people, but not other dogs. Initially, the dogs went to different corners of the field so there was no problem with interference. Sadie calmly worked the field, she was excited to be out there as usual but seemed to have a plan. She wasn't running wildly about nor was she sticking too close to Mary Ann. Judges don't seem to like dogs that won't venture out from their handler.

Sadie took only a few minutes to find a bird. The point was good and she got credit for the bird. A few minutes later she had her second bird. Sadie was on point and Mary Ann was approaching her from the right. Before Mary Ann had a chance to get there, the GSP pup came running between Sadie and the bird. It hesitated briefly and then kept going. I have heard that this is not a huge deal in a junior hunt test, although the GSP probably lost points for this breach. The important thing was that Sadie never broke point, she didn't even flinch. This seemed to sufficiently impress the judges that Sadie was done. Her marks for that test were very high and one judge did some very gratifying gushing later that day. I'm glad the judges didn't see us leaving the field because after I had Sadie back on the leash we happened to walk by a covey of about six quail. Sadie made a beeline for these birds and almost yanked my arm off. I thought I was going to have to carry her out of there. Her bird instincts were cranked up to ten. It's like she knew the test was over and now it was time to eat.

Grace went out and had a pretty routine test. The junior hunt test was not challenging to her. The only real trouble Grace had was, at that point in her life, she wasn't quite convinced that she couldn't catch these birds herself. Being only a little over a year old, she still had pieces of the hunting puzzle to put together. Plus there were a bunch of dogs here that she had never pushed. She was much more interested in the other dog's than Sadie had been. These dogs all needed to know who was boss and once the test was over, Grace was going to start handing out some lessons. Unfortunately, it was getting late in the day and the rest of us voted for a nap.

Grace's scores were also high. Almost as high as Sadie's. Later I looked at a lot of the qualifying scores that had been laid out on a table with the ribbons. There were no other scores as high as our dogs. I can only assume that Sadie got such high scores for holding her point with a dog running right by her nose. Grace will always get high scores if, as she says, "The judges know what's good for them."

We were very proud and some of the GSP owners warmed up to our dogs when they saw the scores. And some cooled off. Everyone makes an effort to be extra nice at events like this. We are, after all, among people with which we have lots in common. But, there was an undercurrent of competition running through most people. I had felt it myself and it's unnecessary. I wanted our dogs to do well, but I wanted all the dogs to do well. The most gracious people we met were the old timers. They'd seen a lot of hunt tests. They'd seen good times and bad. It takes some experience to understand that the important thing was that we were out here hunting with our dogs. They knew that even the ribbons didn't matter. It's nice to listen to those kinds of sentiments. It helped me keep things in perspective. I wanted to do some victory laps and maybe a big burn out with the truck. But, a quieter celebration was more appropriate.

I can see their point but I have to admit I wanted those ribbons and what they represented. We walked out with four ribbons that weekend and both dogs got two crucial legs of their junior hunter accomplished.

Two weeks later we returned to the same location and the dogs officially got their junior hunter titles. We tried to keep them from getting inflated ego's but it was no use. Or maybe that was my own ego.

I had a really good time at the hunt tests we attended. If it's not fun then there's not much reason to go. If you allow yourself to get too competitive and give the ribbon too much importance then you've missed the point.

The people that send their dogs to hunt tests with professional handlers are missing out. They want the title, like I did, but aren't there to participate in it, for whatever reason. The best circumstance would be for every dog to be handled by their owner. Since that isn't possible we get the next best thing.

I did see people there that had dogs being handled by professionals. They didn't have the time or skills to do it themselves but were at least interested enough to go and watch. Not everyone is as devoted to their dogs and hunting as Mary Ann.

In the end, I don't have a problem with what any of these

different categories of people are doing. They are each supporting the hunting dog club in one way or another and that's very important. These clubs operate on the edge financially. I doubt any of them are making much money so they will take any contribution they can get.

It's certainly easy to see how someone could get carried away with collecting ribbons. Ribbons show the world that you have a dog with skills. They are easy to display. They grab your attention with their bright colors and shiny words. Many people hang them on the dog's kennel. That's great as long as you don't put too much emphasis on the ribbon. I keep telling myself that because I want to miss the point and put too much emphasis on the ribbon.

Most people quickly get over the initial excitement of winning a ribbon. They act like adults and don't get carried away with it. That's not what I would do. Mary Ann has all of Sadie and Graces' ribbons in a closet somewhere. I don't think she has looked at them since they won them. Conversely, I would have them mounted in a sort of shrine for all visitors to see. I'd like a small spotlight, one for each dog, that swiveled back and forth across all the many ribbons. It wouldn't have to be visible from the highway, that would be tacky. It's important to keep your dog shrine tasteful. Make sure you provide enough information so that people understand the importance of what they are seeing. People don't like to read little signs like in a museum so I'd go with a series of loud speakers for extra clarity. The pre-recorded message would play in a loop and give onlookers all the details about each ribbon and the triumph that each one represented.

The only disappointing thing about our hunt tests is that there were no protestors. It seems like everything I do is unpopular with someone. Usually the more fun it is, the more someone else doesn't like it. So, a few angry protestors would have been nice, if just to confirm to me that these hunt tests are providing a certain level of fun.

Gas

I don't want anyone to buy a Weimaraner based on something I said. I love these dogs and it would be easy to interpret that as an endorsement to go out and get your own. If you are thinking "These dogs sound great, let's get one." Then stop, because that would be a mistake. I'm not trying to talk anyone into owning a Weimaraner. I'm actually trying to talk people out of it.

I'm not sure "owner" is the correct term for this relationship anyway. This is more of a partnership where one party pays all the bills and the other sleeps a lot and brings back a bird once in a while.

It's not as if these dogs aren't dangerous to own. The world needs to be warned that I put my life on the line every time I go to sleep in the same house as these dogs. They're not vicious but they have a habit of stinking up the place to such a degree that lives are at risk. These dogs have a lot of gas. A lot. Weimaraner's have a lot of gas like Exxon has a lot of gas. It's not a good idea to smoke around these dogs. I wouldn't light a gas stove around them either. I get nervous turning on the propane in the camper.

I've seen some people try to make excuses, "Hey that's not unusual, lots of dog's have gas." Some people try to pretend it isn't happening, "I don't smell anything." Right before they pass out. And some people tell me I must be exaggerating. These people have never had their nasal cavity set on fire by Weimaraner wind.

The gas producing capabilities of these dogs defies several laws of physics and thermodynamics. I can't explain it scientifically, no one can. I just know there's a lot more gas in there than there should be. Weimaraner's use this excess gas as a test to see who their real friends are. Only people that love them would keep these stinkers around after a few high pressure releases.

I had thought again that Sadie was just an exceptional dog in this regard. She can pop off a little smoker to get more room on the couch or she can clear a room if she wants privacy. She seemed uniquely talented. Then we got Grace and we found that it wasn't just Sadie, it's a gift of the breed.

Grace doesn't give up anything to Sadie in any of the major competitive gas categories including hang time, average stench, or the long distance metrics. I realized very quickly that there was about to be a gas war in our living room as both dogs fought for the title Queen of the Fog.

They go toe to toe in a doggy stink off that has injured the nose and offended the sensibilities of more than one innocent bystander. But, as Sadie has said on more than one occasion, "Only those who produce no gas are innocent." And there is some truth to that I guess.

In fact though, if you aren't ok with having all the hair in your nose burned out by a cute little flame thrower, then these aren't the dogs for you. You might want to go with a smaller, safer dog, with less combustion.

One of the interesting things about animals in general is that each has its own distinctive personality. Each Weimaraner has its own distinctive gas delivery method. Sadie likes to sidle up next to me, raise an eyebrow, and say, "Hey Ken, pull my finger." And I always fall for it and she lays down a room full of cloud cover. She can clear a room quicker than a politician collecting money. And she's such a proud dog prancing around the room and claiming ownership, "That one's mine!"

Grace takes a completely different approach. She's not one to ask permission or give advanced warning, she's favors the sneak attack. Grace puts her back feet on the couch and her front feet on the floor, then makes a long stretch and blasts out a four note song called "Here come the tears." Then she raises her back foot up in a final flourish, toot toot. It's a signature style all her own.

Sadie and Grace, whom we like to call Thunder and Lightning, don't require any special food to brew up these concoctions. Anything seems to work fine. The raw materials don't seem to matter at all. Some people say "Hey put them on a low gas diet." What's that supposed to mean? All they eat is dog food. No matter what goes in, you know what comes out.

Each Weimaraner comes with a patented German gas process that is guaranteed to create paint peeling masterpieces for a lifetime. Apparently, Weimaraner's get better at this as they get older and hone their skills to a sharp edge. Practice makes perfect.

There are certain safety tips that you can use to keep your household damage to a minimum. No one alerted us to any of these procedures; we learned them all the hard way. First, if you find yourself lost in a Weimaraner cloud bank and you feel dizzy or begin to lose consciousness, remove yourself to fresh air immediately (assuming you can still walk). If you find there is no fresh air, you've been the victim of a full house bombing, try to get outside. Always touch the door knob before opening any doors. The room you are moving into may already have been lit up.

If you are successful in making your escape to the outside and still have no breathable air, you may have to make a run for it. Remember to leave your dog in the house. In their panic, some Weimaraner owners try to "rescue" their dogs. This is like taking the arsonist with you when your house is on fire. These dogs don't appear to need to breathe anyway and they will just keep blasting you until you pass out.

It is possible you will have to run a quarter to a half mile or more before you are clear. I heard about two old Weimaraner's that got into some smoked gouda and rendered an entire neighborhood uninhabitable for days. But, that is worst case and probably won't happen to you. When you get to a safe zone you may want to put up some of that yellow perimeter tape. Your neighbors will appreciate it.

In the unlikely event that your clothes actually catch fire, remember to stop, drop, and roll.

These are extreme cases of course. Usually you will just have a localized brown out. You may just want to hold your breath until someone sounds the all clear. Most Weimaraner owners can hold their breath for several minutes or more due to repeated exposures and daily practice.

Some damage is unavoidable. You are going to lose your lawn. On occasion, our front yard experiences a double detonation and is off limits until the smoke clears. You can see the blast zones where our grass was burned up in triangle patterns. Another casualty is carpet. They don't make carpet that can take this pounding. Our carpet was like walking on bubble wrap until we got rid of it. Leftover pockets of Weimaraner gas would pop as you went room to room. I would recommend linoleum, pressure treated wood, or concrete as the best flooring. Linoleum generally doesn't burn, you just get some melted spots in it. It makes an interesting pattern.

We considered building an underground bunker as a safety refuge. Kind of like the bomb shelters of the 1950's and the survivalist set ups they have these days.We were going to stock it with a full complement of masks and chemical suits. But, we figured Sadie and Grace would find a way in and you don't want to be in a confined space with these two right after dinner time. So, we ditched that idea. Sadie has figured out how to open zippers so locked doors seem like only a matter of time.

One of the favorite pastimes of dog owner's is checking out the new batches of puppy pictures on the Internet. They are all so cute it makes me (briefly) want to get another one. These are scenes of adorable Weimaraner happiness but I bet it sounds like firecrackers popping on the Fourth of July. I've never seen Weimaraner breeders wearing respirators in those pictures but they probably are just out of camera range.

For new Weimaraner owners a help group has been established to assist in dealing with uncontrolled releases and the inevitable "first timer" panic. Many of the fears that the new puppy is "choking the children", "melting the furniture", or "killing us" can be quickly diffused. This team fields all sorts of panic calls and a team of fog experts is standing by to alleviate your stinky dog concerns. Call the Department of Gas, Fast Action Rescue Team. This is not another government agency, it's a band of civilian freedom fighters dedicated to clean survivable air and happy dog owners.

Finally I'd like to warn you about a condition called turd certain. It's a state of mind that will be familiar to Weimaraner owners. It's that feeling that a certain dog has done a certain something in the wrong place.

Once in a while, too often if you ask me, Sadie or Grace will deliver a little gift that seems to have more substance than should be possible for mere gas. This creates a moment of temporary panic called turd certain. This is when you smell something that you are sure has crossed the line from harmless gas to something more solid. And let's be clear, you don't just suspect that there's a turd in the room, you don't "have a feeling" there's a turd in the room, you know it. You are Turd Certain.

It first happened to me one night while I was fast asleep. I suddenly became totally awake when the smell hit me like a punch in the nose. I tried to get the light on as fast as I could thinking, "Man, that is really close, Sadie must have gone right in the bed! Maybe she's sick, maybe she was trying to tell me and I didn't wake up, geez I can't breathe!" all in the space of five seconds. Then I got the light on and expected a terrible mess but I just found Sadie pointing at the cat saying "There's something wrong with that cat." And I briefly considered that it could have been the cat, but no, future carnage confirmed the true culprit.

There's been a natural evolution in the conversations around our house in light of the many Weimaraner bombings. A stranger would think we were crazy if they were to walk in and hear us grading the various efforts by these dogs. We're all very competitive around here so of course we've made it into a sport. I never expected to be an amateur fart judge but nothing could be more normal. We're just adapting to the reality of living with Weimaraner's. You may not know the difference between a nose burner, a belly turner, or a turd certain championship winner, but you will in just a few short weeks with these dogs.

Sometimes I think maybe I'm being too sensitive. It's like Sadie says, "Stop being a baby, it wasn't that bad." But, it's hard to sit on the couch with your eyes watering and not think your choice of dog could have been better. We've considered that this might be a ploy to get us to take them outside. I imagine them thinking "Alright, maybe this one will get you off the couch." But, despite a house full of turd certain people, many trips to the yard have resulted in no action other than me and a dog watching cars go by.

Of course, any breed of dog can have a breezy personality like Weimaraner's, so it's not fair to judge them too harshly. The important thing is that they have many positive qualities to offset this one. And it's good to open all your windows and even evacuate your neighborhood once in a while, even in winter. It get's everyone out of the house for a little exercise, and that's a good thing.

Animal Psychiatry

I once took our cat to the vet because he was getting old and acting erratic. He wasn't eating well and was no longer interested in the litter box. This has spelled doom for many cats throughout history and eventually was our own cat's downfall as well. But, that was much later. At this point we were thinking the vet could still fix him.

The vet said, "Maybe something is bothering him." I said I didn't know but I guess it's possible. I know his peeing on the kitchen floor is bothering me. Actually, we had thought that he might be trying to tell us something. We had tried some things like getting a new box and changing to different litter. And nothing had worked. So I stopped thinking about what might be on the cat's mind and decided that maybe he had some physical issue that made using the box an impossibility. I wouldn't have brought him to the vet If I had thought he was just upset about something.

The checkup went well, he seemed healthy for a twelve year old cat. The vet however, went back to his state of mind and started asking me all kinds of questions about the cat's daily "pressures". I said, "Well, he sleeps all night with a couple of Weimaraners and then gets up to whiz on the kitchen floor. Then he grabs his morning dog kibble out of the bowl for a snack and heads back to bed for 18 to 20 hours." But, that wasn't enough information for the vet and she proceeded with more questions. I then realized, to my shock and horror, that we were analyzing this cat like a couple of animal psychiatrists. I'm extremely doubtful about the value of analyzing people, much less cats. I don't know if the vet really thought I was going to help her figure out what weighing on the cat's mind or not but I wasn't much help. I figure if a cat has plenty of food and water, a clean box, and a safe place to sleep all day, then nothing should be bothering it. I really think that's a cat's "best case life".

Finally she got to the dog question. Do the Weimaraner's bother the cat? Yes, I'm quite sure the Weimaraner's bother the cat. At least some of the time. The Weimaraner's would love to chase the cat all over the house but he won't run from them. I've never seen either Weimaraner retrieve the cat and bring it back to me in its mouth. Then again, I've never asked them to. Grace of course gives everyone that challenges her authority a push now and then. And since the cat dwells within her realm, Grace crowds him every so often. But, the cat quickly learned to ignore her until she goes away. I once heard the cat say, "Yes your majesty you are the dominant dog here, what a fine beast you are, yawn."

Grace drinks water out of her bowl using the tsunami method. I suppose she must actually drink some of the water but most of it goes over the side in waves. I have witnessed that cat standing up on his hind legs drinking from the other side of the bowl. An intimidated cat just wouldn't do that. That was the last time I worried about whether the dogs bothered him.

The only benefit I see in animal psychology is in gaining a general knowledge of how they think. This would certainly help in training hunting dogs. I would bet that all dog trainers spend some time learning and thinking about how dogs think because that helps to understand how they will react to certain situations and how you can influence them.

The biggest problem with dog psychology is that I can't get the picture of Sadie on the shrink's couch out of my head. If a doctor ever got Sadie on their couch they'd have a tough time limiting her to the usual one hour session. She just starts to get comfortable in an hour.

That made me start thinking about how things would actually go if dog psychiatry was real and if Sadie could really talk and if I would pay for her to go see a head shrinker.

I'd bet it would go something like this. I've translated Sadie's responses from dog into English.

Shyster: Well Sadie how are things going?

Sadie: I tell you it's been tough around the house lately doc. They bought some treats that I just don't care for and apparently I'm going to have to eat the whole bag anyway.

And speaking of treats, Ken is especially stingy with those things. You'd think he'd get the message and bring home thirty or forty bags of them. I've been to that store, I know the supply is there. One time he asked what kind of treats I wanted, I said get them all Mr. treat miser. Fill up five or six carts and let's clean this place out. But, he ignored me and got two measly bags.

And let's talk about the naps around here. I'm no prima donna, I'll sleep anywhere, all I need is a bed and a pillow, and sometimes a blanket. What is the big deal about needing a pillow? I don't see any of you people sleeping without a pillow. And would it kill them to fluff these pillows once in a while? One time I tossed and turned on an unfluffed pillow for almost a whole minute. This is relevant because my sleep is important. I'm not a normal dog, I'm a hunting dog, I've got ribbons to prove it. I can't get out to the field and say well, I can't find birds today because my sleep was substandard. I'm under a lot of pressure.

And speaking of treats, why do we spend so much time away from them. We go to the farm at least once a day to patrol and make sure things are safe. It's a ton of responsibility. Does anyone pack treats for the good dogs on this trip? Of course not, so why is it so shocking that I'm going to look for some alternate treat source? I have to supplement my diet somehow. From their reaction you'd think I ate the last ear of corn off the field. What I'm doing is sampling. A farm is where they grow food. And with certain menu selections you just can't tell if it's food until after you eat it. I'm not the first dog to have said this. I'm not making this up. It's proven dog lore. Have mistakes been made? Absolutely, I can't vouch for things that smell like food but actually aren't. But worrying about car seats is so petty. As if a little puke on the car seat matters in the big picture.

After a hot run around the farm I like to cool my undercarriage in the stream. It's not my fault there's dirt at the bottom of the stream. I wish the stream was lined with treats. Judging by his reaction you'd think Ken had never seen dirt (or whatever) on a dog before. He always asks me how I got so filthy and I say didn't you just see me rolling in "dirt" (or whatever) over there? But, he ignores me as usual. This is what I deal with everyday!

And let's talk about this whole hunting thing. I have to admit I'm pretty into it. But, let me tell you, hunting with Mary Ann is a results oriented activity. And it's quite thankless as well. At the end of the day they'll say something like, "We got four birds." They never say, "Well Sadie found twelve birds and we only got four didn't we Ken? Wonder why we only got four out of twelve Ken?" And here's a question for you, if I found twelve birds then I wonder why I didn't get twelve treats? Someone that bad at math shouldn't be in charge of the treats. I'm telling you it's a pressure cooker. And unfair as well. The payoff for all that work just isn't there. It's not like they don't have enough pockets to carry enough treats to adequately compensate a dog. I spend most of my time wondering which of their thirty pockets they're hiding the treats.

Then there's hunt tests. They take me to hunt tests and some strangers with no treats grade me on finding birds in a field. Really? How about giving me something difficult like finding a treat in Ken's truck. I could find birds on the surface of the moon. You say there are no birds on the moon? Well I guess the astronauts should have taken a Weimaraner with them if they wanted to find birds. Ken couldn't find a bird in the meat section of a grocery store. And why take a visually stunning dog such as Grace and myself to a hunt test full of GSP's? As if I don't hear everyone whispering "They're visually stunning but it's a shame what's been done to the Weimaraner." As if we don't always walk out with all the ribbons. Come on now, this isn't the 1960's, you don't have to be so jealous anymore. Weimaraner's don't have thumbs, we don't answer the phone, and we don't think we're people.

Shyster: Well, looks like our time is up Sadie.

Sadie: Let me give you a scenario doc. Let's say our house faces a security breach. A robber or maybe a bureaucrat breaks down the door of our house. It doesn't matter if it's a daring daylight raid or a night time sneak attack. The Weimaraner's are supposed to be on guard at all times. The intruders take all our snacks, food, and chew toys but the dogs don't bark or put up a fuss at all. Who do you think gets the blame for this unprovoked home intrusion? Not Mr. and Mrs. Hunter that's for sure. The Weimaraner's will take that heat. The Weimaraner's would just like a little clarity about the rules. Instead, we're told to bark at robbers but not at strangers. They want a warning about intruders but guys in brown clothes that drop boxes on our porch and then run away are ok. We deal with so many mixed messages and contradictory instructions I need a scorecard to keep track. I guess I shouldn't expect so much of people. They're doing their best I guess. The best thing to do is treat them with a lick and a wag.

By the way doc, you got any treats in this office? You know, to help with the therapy. No? Hm, ok.

So anyway, Grace and I do all we can to protect our house from robbers, dog nappers, tax collectors, and other household threats. I trained Grace to go loud early and often. It's too hard to tell the difference between the guy delivering the newspaper (good) and the guy selling newspaper subscriptions (bad). Don't bother waiting for permission to bark at robbers, you won't get it. It's easier to get forgiveness than permission. So go crazy first and face the consequences later. You can always say, "Hey, my bad, thought that was a robber." After they stop yelling at you they'll thank you.

Shyster: Let's save something for next time Sadie.

Sadie: If I know Ken doc, there won't be a next time. Better let me get it all out now. Do you have any siblings doc? I have a few but we don't speak. It's not an issue because we were never close. I prefer people anyway. But, let me tell you about Grace, the latest addition to our pack. I don't know where she gets her information but she's an opinionated little dog. Grace is quite sure that Mary Ann likes her best and that Ken's place in the pack is up for discussion. Now, I'm a laid back, relaxed kind of dog. Like a Hawaiimaraneran. So, I'm not stressing about who likes who the best. As long as the treats flow like water and every chair has a cushion, I'm fine. But, I worry about Ken. To say he doesn't pay attention would be like saying the sky is blue. He's so ripe for a coup it's ridiculous. When Grace makes her move he won't know what hit him. I won't support her though. Grace has an agenda that includes very few naps. And I don't think the treat ratio would favor me if she ever got promoted to management. Like I said, I'm not a political dog, I like a nice quiet house. If she wants to get upwardly mobile on us then she's on her own.

As you can see, Sadie would be an ideal patient for a

doctor being paid by the hour. That motor mouth could probably go on for days. I'm just glad this is a hypothetical scenario. The last thing we need around here is a bunch of bills for Weimaraner therapy.

This example clearly demonstrates why I could never be this kind of therapist. The thought of listening to someone's alleged problems and then being expected to somehow solve them is my idea of torture. Even for money I'd have a tough time with it. I guess that's why it costs a lot of money. I'm afraid I give out rather unhelpful answers like, "Wow, you're messed up." or "I thank my lucky stars nothing like that has ever happened to me." or "Let me stop you right there, we need to move right to the prescription drug phase of this therapy." Maybe I'm putting too much stress on the problem solving. That doesn't seem to be the main focus from of this sort of therapy.

I can't imagine any scenario in which Grace allows herself to be analyzed. It just wouldn't go well. She wouldn't gain anything from it and the doctor wouldn't enjoy it either. Two minutes into her session, she'd be ruining the doctor's day. Grace isn't afraid to say, "You're not very good at this." or "A professional therapist would offer refreshments." She's a straight shooter and a backseat driver. I can also imagine her saying, "So I'm supposed to tell you what's bothering me and then you tell me how to fix it? Or will you give me some nonsense about empowerment and I still have to fix it myself?"

Grace's bird obsession would undoubtedly come up in a therapy session. But, she doesn't see it as a problem. The problem she sees is that everyone isn't equally obsessed. She'd likely try to talk the doctor into taking her hunting. "It's easy. I'll find the birds, you just shoot them when they fly. Then you cook them up and give them back to me. Don't put too much breading on my pheasant."

The science of understanding dog behavior is real. There are enough people writing books about it that there must be something to it. I'm just not sure about the goals. If you want to use science to find out what dog's are thinking and predict they're behavior, good luck.

Watching how dogs behave is one of my hobbies. There's no doubt that a person that took the time to become an animal behaviorist will not see things the way I do. So, I'm not telling scientists they shouldn't write their books. But, nearly all these books take the subject too seriously. That's a common problem with scientists.

You can't learn how to create a great relationship with your dog by reading a book on the subject. You have to be there every day, making mistakes and renewing your commitment to each other. Information is great, just don't depend too much on what you read in books. Shortcuts can cause more problems than they solve. In the end you still have to do the hard work, you still have to pick up the poop.

Some scientists have suggested that I anthropomorphize my Weimaraner's. Which means that I pretend they are people. And that isn't helpful in furthering dog behavior science. That's probably true. It doesn't take a scientist to realize that I'm no scientist. Of course I anthropomorphize Sadie and Grace, the alternative is to treat them as test subjects. And that get's boring quickly.

At first I thought that these dog scientists were wasting their time studying such an unfathomable subject. Then I realized how brilliant they are. The study of dog behavior is the perfect scientific subject. They get to play with their dog all day and call it work. They have fun writing books of varying value but make no final conclusions because none are possible. More study will always be needed. We'll always be looking for that definitive study that answers the final question about dog behavior.

Scientific studies show that you can prove nearly anything. Unscientific studies show that scientific studies don't solve any problems. So, although I'm glad there is a thriving community of people dedicated to figuring out how dog's think, I'm skeptical about the value of the endeavor. When I read dog behavior books, I very often enjoy the entire thing, then disregard everything in it. I'm happy to have the author's opinion, but if it's nonsense then it has to be categorized as such.

It is, obviously, my hope that the study of dog behavior will continue for a long time to come. Let's all agree to continue writing books that delve into the mystery that is the dog mind.

Camping

We've all seen those big campers and RV's barreling down the highway. I never paid much attention to them unless they were in my way. It seems like they are all going too fast or too slow. These things were just huge anonymous white blocks to me.

Then, we bought one. Now, I see all the different kinds. I pick out the models we almost bought, I see the features we didn't get, I see the one's we might get next. Sometimes I see our exact camper and beep at them.

I thought our model was rare. They were discontinuing the line so it seemed like we'd be unique. I didn't want to see a bunch of our same camper at the campground. And we don't. But, I still see it on the road quite a bit. It's the same way with cars. Buy a car that you think is uncommon because you never see it and you'll see tons of them in the first week.

If I had any thoughts about campers before we had one, it was always to wonder why on earth anyone would go to that much trouble for camping. I hadn't been camping much in my life. I had all the negatives in my mind, it was hot, I wouldn't be able to sleep, there's bugs, there's nothing to do, if it rains you are stuck in a camper, the bathroom facilities are questionable. I never stopped to think that there might be an experience good enough to make all those negatives tolerable.

The secret is that camping is actually worth all that trouble. And RV camping is twice as good as tent camping. We thought the RV would be a great way to get away and enjoy the outdoors. And it is, but it's much better than I thought it would be. It gives me distance from "to do" lists. It's surprising how important it is to have something different to look at and think about than the usual. They call it "recharging your batteries" I guess. I never liked that term so I don't call it that.

We've had issues mixing hotels and Weimaraner's. When you tow your own hotel room, no one gets to tell you that they don't allow dogs. Unless the campground doesn't allow dogs. Or if it discriminates against certain kinds of dogs.

Some people don't enjoy camping, probably because they don't hate their jobs enough. I thought I didn't like my job, but I had no idea how much until I spent a weekend camping and then had to go back to work on Monday. Maybe I wouldn't enjoy camping as much if I didn't have such a terrible job. But, I'd like to find out.

One of the unexpected pleasures of camping is that it feels like you are getting away with something. I'll never forget the day I took the camper home. I couldn't believe they were going to let me drive this thing out on the road. I got very few instructions from the dealer. They hooked it up, slapped me on the back and said, "We're here if you wreck it." I pulled away from the RV dealership with no idea how I was going to get this thing home. I was anxious but it was oddly liberating. It felt like freedom. It felt like I was closer to making the most of life. If I had known it would be anything like this I'd have been out driving class A motor homes all the time.

I knew it was legal because I saw other campers on the road. But, it didn't feel legal. It felt like I was breaking the law. I couldn't see much behind me. The mirrors seemed small and the camper seemed huge. Mary Ann was in her car behind me. We figured she could help by letting me over if necessary. But, I couldn't see her. There were a lot of other cars around, but I couldn't see them or avoid them, they'd have to watch out for me. And the cops didn't care, they passed me right by, ignoring the chance to remove an obvious road menace. I felt like a hazard to public safety. But, I was finally the guy people looked at and said, "Look at this guy, doing whatever he wants. Not a care in the world for the carnage he might cause."

The only possible problem was making a wrong turn and having to somehow turn the camper around. Turning around held the possibility of using reverse, something I had no intention of doing. The RV dealer was in an unfamiliar part of town, I'd been there twice, so my idea of how to get home was vague. I knew I was looking for I 95 but couldn't remember the turns I needed to make. I saw the exit late and swerved over, hoping that Mary Ann was over there creating some space. Somehow I merged onto I 95 and I began to relax. Which is bizarre, because I've never felt relaxed on that road before. I knew there was nothing to do but drive straight for a while. And at least I knew the way home from there. As the cars whizzed by me, I settled back into my seat and thought about all the times a camper had gotten in my way. Now, I was the one going ten miles under the speed limit. I was the one making late lane changes because I didn't know where I was going. And it was a fantastic, liberating feeling. I sped up to nearly 55 mph. Then I remembered the limit was 65 here. I wasn't sure the camper would hold together at that speed but I thought, "Why not?". Throwing caution to the wind I got to the posted speed and probably went a little over. I may have gone as fast as 70 mph that day.

That first drive would have been considerably more difficult without Mary Ann driving blocker in her car. I realized that she was the Bandit and I was the Snowman. And that made things even better.

We got our travel trailer, which is not one of the huge ones, the year after Sadie was born. So, she's been camping for as long as she can remember. She's a seasoned camper who knows all the tricks for getting some "off the leash" time. We learned quickly that campgrounds do not allow dogs to be off the leash, at all. The reasons are obvious but they don't make much sense to Sadie.

One of our first trips was to a state park called Tuckahoe. The campground at the park features large wooded sites and none of the usual campground amenities like cable tv or zip lines. Most people seem to go there for the lake. They allow some swimming and fishing so during the day most of the campers are at the lake enjoying the water.

They do have a flying disc golf course. The kind where you hit some hanging chains and hope the disc falls in the basket. I guess this could be considered a quasi-amenity. I had no intention of playing because it seemed so childish, yet difficult. Two hours later I was at the disc golf course showing Mary Ann and Sadie how it was done. It was deserted while everyone was at the lake so we had no trouble getting on the course. Not surprisingly, Sadie loves flying disc golf, even though she rarely scores a point. Her strategy is mostly defensive. I throw the disc, Sadie keeps it from going into the goal. It works for her but is boring to watch. People like offense.

Tuckahoe has the usual leash rules. They are not unreasonable and campers know not to let their dogs roam free. In fact, the only dog I saw off the leash that whole weekend was Sadie. She snapped the check cord that I had tied to a tree and took off for an unsupervised trip through the campground. Surprisingly, there were no rangers around to see her.

In the ongoing quest for "off the leash" time, we decided to go for a hike. There was no one on the trail with us so off the leash she went. As I said before this is highly illegal, especially in Maryland. If you don't enjoy lectures, fines, threats of dog confiscation, arrests, and other legal procedures then don't let your dog off the leash, ever.

Once again, our judgment proved sound and we had an enjoyable hike. We got back to the camper only to discover why there was no one on that trail. Apparently everyone knew about that trail but us. It's where ticks go for their summer vacation. I expect to find a tick or two when after I spend all day in the woods, but I brushed whole families of ticks off my clothes. We spent the next hour and a half getting ticks off Sadie. I've never seen such a variety of ticks on one dog. In fact, I've never seen such a variety anywhere. We had to use olive oil to get some of them off, especially the little ones between her toes. It was difficult but we all smelled like olive oil for a while so that was good. I doubt that anyone ever goes on that trail twice. I don't know how many total ticks there were but it was enough to rename the park Tickahoe.

I felt a lot better about breaking their leash law after that. None of the rangers we talked to warned us about the tick hike. And surely they must have known. A little warning would have been nice.

We achieved a new level of appreciation for our RV at a state park called Rocky Gap. We happened to be there on the same weekend as a major car show. First off, we took the mandatory hike around the lake. There was minimal "off the leash" time due to the woods being filled with children. Sadie got hugs from children half her size. When the hike was over, we walked over to look at the cars. There were hundreds of old cars there. I am amazed at the amount of work people put into fixing up these cars. No wonder they take them out to show off.

Sadie was on the leash walking next to Mary Ann when a guy walked up to us and asked how we got her to do that. He was a new Weimaraner owner that could not get his dog to calmly walk next to him. His Weimaraner wouldn't calmly do anything. He was shocked to see a Weimaraner on a leash and not pulling the owner across the ground. Part of the secret is to take your Weimaraner on a two hour hike through the woods. Getting rid of the excess energy promotes calmness. All three of us were exhausted and looking forward to some sitting around the campfire time. The other part is that Sadie wasn't on a regular leash, she was on a command lead. This is a stiff piece of rope that is a better choice for training than a normal six foot leash. It fits differently than a regular leash and gives the dog a better feel for what the leash holder is trying to do.

After looking at cars for a while we returned to camp. Little did we know there would be no campfire that night. It started raining when we got back to the camper and didn't stop all night. There were biblical amounts of rain falling. I saw tents float past our site. Out in the elements it was one nasty night. Inside the RV it was a different world. We were dry and cool. Sadie crawled in bed and napped until bedtime. The waterproof roof was taking a beating but did it's job tremendously. We cooked dinner on the propane stove and toasted the inventor of the RV. While the winds lashed the outside of the camper, Mary Ann baked cookies in the oven. I looked out the window and saw that all the tent campers had packed up and gone home. The park would be a lot less crowded tomorrow.

Every piece of wood we had was wet at a molecular level. We never got a fire started the whole weekend. I had hidden our wood under the camper but it rained there too. The park had no dry wood to sell because their wood shed had no roof on it. Whenever anyone ever mentions the virtues of tent camping to me I think of this weekend. They say that tent camping is the only true camping. Sleeping in an RV is cheating. I just smile and agree with them.

Grace was also camping at a young age. So she knows the drill and is nearly a perfect camping dog. She doesn't bark at other campers or try to run off by herself. She asks for permission before she pushes other dogs around. As long as she can see and approve of all the activities going on, she's fine.

When we're all outside we like to put a dog bed on the ground and stake out Sadie and Grace so they can be in the middle of the fun. Inevitably people will start coming by and asking what kind of dogs they are. It's like a couple of rock stars at an autograph signing. They practically have a receiving line. All the attention doesn't go to Grace's head, she's very level headed. I'm not sure about Sadie though, she's more likely to get a big ego.

Grace prefers state parks to the more commercialized campgrounds. She doesn't care about water and sewer hookups and she doesn't watch much TV. Plus there are fewer opportunities for "off the leash" time at the big busy places. They cater to families, not to dogs. Grace's ideal campground would not allow leashes. And there would be no campers allowed without dogs. Each night all the dogs would gather around a big fire and Grace would preside over the proceedings from her raised dais. If you are going to dream you might as well dream big.

We had a great time camping at a state park up in the Catskill Mountains of New York. It was a beautiful place with great views of the mountains and a fifteen acre pond with a beach for small kids. The lake was so clear I could almost see to the bottom of it. That's how I know there were no fish in there.

We decided to try some fishing anyway. We bought licenses but didn't catch anything. I don't know why they sell licenses if they know the lake is empty. I guess the bigger question is why anyone buys licenses when you can see almost to the bottom of the lake. Maybe we are eternal optimists, I don't know. Since we didn't know exactly what kind of fish were theoretically in the pond we used bait to accommodate both small trout and huge trout. It didn't matter what we used, nothing had a chance.

One big plus to fishing this weekend, despite not catching anything, was that we got some use out of our amazing folding canoe. This is one of those plastic canoes that folds up to something like six inches wide. Every time I get in it I can't help wondering when it will finally collapse and send us swimming back to shore. However, once again, it didn't sink. That's all I ask of that canoe. Anything more would be pushing my luck. It is a miracle of canoe engineering that keeps this thing afloat. Maybe I'm more conscious about my lack of swimming skills than I should be. But, paddling around in a canoe that was folded up in the back of the truck five minutes ago made me very aware that my position above water was precarious. I knew that if the boat collapsed I'd probably have to be towed back to shore by a Weimaraner. And we were way out there too. There were times when I thought it would be a long walk back to shore, forget about swimming it.

The camp sites at this park were generally small for parking a twenty six foot camper. There were only a handful that I would have even a remote chance of getting into. By some miracle Mary Ann had picked one of the only ones that was big enough. And still it wasn't easy to get the camper in there. Most of the campers were in tents and I got the impression that they didn't get many RV's in this park. It was cool to have the biggest camper in the park for once. There wasn't a Montana in sight.

Once we got the camper parked the site was great, as most state park sites are. What they lack in hookups they make up for in privacy and plenty of space. We made a fire the first night and went into hard relax mode.

The drive up to New York had been difficult because we had to drive all the way through Pennsylvania. It was the Friday before July 4th so I expected some congestion. I didn't expect every road in PA to be jammed. The problem with Pennsylvania is that they put it right next to Maryland, so if I go north at all, it's difficult to avoid. It's a wide state with narrow roads. To say PA was having a bad traffic day is an understatement. It was stop and go almost all the way. We got a six hour education in bad road design that we didn't want or need.

On the plus side we did come up with solutions to every road problem in PA. First, they have too many cars. Get rid of some or don't allow new ones to be registered. A two year moratorium on new cars would probably do it. Second, the on ramps are only ten feet long. No driver whose name isn't Dale Earnhardt can merge in only ten feet. So, backups and accidents inevitably ensue. Make the on ramps longer or get rid of them. Third, there's a red light ten feet down every off ramp. And it only turns green once a day. Get rid of all lights at the end of off ramps. Fourth, build separate roads for big trucks. I don't want to see any big trucks. Trucks are always getting in my way. When I'm towing a camper, nothing should be going slower than me. The only time I should see big trucks is if I'm using their special roads because the car roads are all backed up. Fifth, smooth these roads out a little. I shouldn't have to wonder if the camper is going to detach from the truck because the road has a crater in it. I'm going to type up all these solutions and send them to the governor. That way it will all be fixed when we go back through there.

The state park in New York had a very stringent recycling

policy. They are saving the planet one bottle at a time there. The only thing they didn't have a receptacle for was bags of dog poop. Of which I had an abundant supply.

We weren't looking to do too much on this trip so we did a lot of relaxing. Which is how camping should be. There's no need for a lot of activities until you get tired of what you can see from your chair by the fire.

The park was able to meet our low standards but only scored a three out of ten on the Weimaraner camping scale. The possibility of "off the leash" time was low. My conclusion was that this was due to subtle government oppression of Weimaraner's. Grace gave the park a point for having the possibility of encountering a bear. Most people don't want to see a bear in their campsite, Grace is convinced she could win a stare down with a bear, especially one of these small eastern black bears. She asks for a bear for her birthday every year. Sadie gave the park a point for having so many small children asking the magic question, "Can I pet your dog?". She doesn't care how nervous it makes me. Both dogs gave the park a half point for having so many "interesting" smells. I've never been able to understand how the smell scale works. I think it has to do with the fact that my nose barely functions after repeated exposure to Weimaraner gas. Still, these dogs discover/cause some very odd smells that stagger me and don't seem to faze them at all.

And they supposedly have this bionic nose. I can't figure it out.

The quest for "off the leash" time seemed to be over. I figured it just wasn't going to happen. The dogs weren't about to accept that answer. While we were fishing, Sadie created her own "off the leash" time by jumping out of the canoe. It was an awkward dismount that needs some work. It was a kind of half dive, half barrel roll. There was a certain degree of difficulty but the execution just wasn't there. I'm sure she will practice as much as we will let her. She jumped out this time with the intention of retrieving the lure that I had just cast out into the water. So her heart was in the right place. She was about as happy with our fishing results as I was. I told her to bring back a trout since the bait I was using didn't seem to be working anyway.

Dogs weren't allowed at the beach or the picnic area. Since the park consisted of a campground, a beach, and a picnic area, that didn't leave us with much choice. There were plenty of helpful signs to remind us of what dogs can't do. There were signs for keeping the dogs on the leash, picking up the "waste", no barking, no growling, no loud water slurping, and no scaring children. They forgot no snoring and no stinking up the camper. I didn't see any signs prohibiting dog swimming out in the middle of the lake. Honestly though, there were so many signs I could have missed it.

Not to be outdone, Grace followed Sadie into the water for some swimming time of her own. We didn't know if there would be fines for this unlicensed swimming so we let them go for a while. I figured the fine would be the same for a one minute swim as it was for an hour long swim. After having no real "off the leash" time for a day, Sadie and Grace were buzzing around the canoe like they had outboard motors.

We had no good way to get them back in the canoe. We had bait but it was for fish. We had a net but it was too small. Mary Ann was in the front of the canoe so she hauled them back in the old fashioned way, one hand on the collar and one hand under the back legs, while I did my best to keep the canoe from flipping over. Two wet gray dogs were all that we caught that day. There were no signs about a catch and release dog program so we did not release them. No ranger visited us with a lecture or a fine for catching dogs without a license, so we did it all over again the next day. I believe we would have developed a precedent of taking the dogs for a swim every day if we had stayed longer. That way I could have used the "But we do it all the time" excuse on the ranger. The more you do something wrong without getting caught, the easier it is to pretend you thought it was ok. Usually, if the rangers don't catch you doing something wrong until the tenth time, they'll just tell you to knock it off instead of writing a ticket. That's not advice for how to conduct yourself in a state park. If you get kicked out it's your own fault.

Back at the camper I was thinking about our fishing expedition. It seemed that there was no real chance to catch any fish in that lake. Maybe there were no fish or maybe the fish were smart because they are under so much pressure.

Not for the first time, I wondered if buying a fishing license that day was a waste of money. Usually, the money for hunting and fishing licenses goes to a good cause. But, while I was standing there in a New York state park, ready to hand over my money to a kid that had no answers, I had to wonder if that was true there. Who knows what New York does with their fishing license money. I would have been just as happy to sit in the canoe, enjoy the sun, the water, and watch the Weimaraner's circle the boat as I was fishing for theoretical fish. Next time I might do just that.

Back home I had been told exactly where the money goes so there was some level of comfort. Then I realized that this is something I have to check on every year, at least. The government is sneaky like that. They will change things as soon as I'm not paying attention. And that happens often. It was a reminder of my responsibility to stay vigilant because the people in charge don't always want the same things I want.

Our longest camping excursion, by miles travelled, was all

the way out to Michigan. We went out there to meet some other Weimaraner owners for a grouse hunt. It was too early in my Weimaraner, hunting, and camping evolution for me to fully appreciate what we got to do on this trip. Plus, I was more than tired out by the fourteen hour trip.

I had no idea that Michigan was so far from Maryland. At least, I had no practical knowledge of what it takes to tow a camper that far. Driving with the camper attached to the truck is a little more stressful than normal driving. There are more things that can go wrong so I always have little checklists running through my mind. What will we do if this goes wrong, what about this, what about that. By the time we got to Michigan I had forgotten all about what can go wrong when towing a camper. I just wanted to be there. I didn't look in the rear view mirror, I didn't worry about holding people up. This was my first lesson that worrying about what can go wrong is pointless. It won't stop things from going wrong. The best thing is to spend some time before the trip making sure you are prepared and then think about more important things. If I had known this before the trip I would have been more concerned about being able to hit a grouse or a woodcock with a shotgun.

We had to cut through Pennsylvania on our trip and as you know it's not my favorite place to drive. We started out very early so I didn't get to see quite as many cars as I have on other trips. After PA we went straight through Ohio. To this day I have never seen a dry Ohio road. It rained the entire time we were there, both ways. For all I know it never stops raining there.

Although I was nearly unconscious when we arrived, Sadie and Grace had slept all the way and were ready to explode. The great advantage to having a state park full of Weimaraner's is that there was very little "on the leash" time. What a great thing to know that the camp sites all around you would be happy to see your Weimaraner's pay a visit.

I don't remember much of the first day at grouse camp. I met some people, met some dogs and went to sleep.

The next day was great. I re-met the people and dogs because I didn't remember them from the previous night, and we drove off to hunt grouse. We had a group so we fanned out in a line and marched straight through the brush. There were so many elk droppings I thought it was inevitable that we would see one. Turns out that you don't just stumble upon a herd of elk.

We flushed a grouse on that first try. I didn't see it and no one got a shot at it. But, that doesn't matter with grouse hunting. I learned that with grouse, seeing one is a victory, having a shot at one is cause for celebration, actually shooting one is probably the highlight of your year.

Later that day we flushed another grouse. I was at the end

of the line this time and the bird flew my way. I had a clear view of it, took a shot, and missed. I can understand why they say getting a legitimate shot at a grouse is such a big event. There were a few things working against me. I was walking through brush so thick that I didn't have room to raise my gun about half the time. I was still not very alert, I had the camper equivalent of jet lag. The grouse flushed at a spot that happened to be open enough for me to take a shot. This bird came screaming by me about twenty five feet ahead. When they say grouse fly fast they don't do it justice. And you can't put any mph measurement on it. It's such a surprise when they flush that it seems much faster than it actually is. I saw it for all of three seconds. The fact that I got the safety off, raised the gun, tracked it a little bit, and got the shot off is still amazing to me because I know what my skill level was at that point. I couldn't have missed it by much. I would guess that I shot behind it. I look back at it and realize it was one of my finest hunting moments. And was surely the finest up to that point.

However, I didn't know then how rare grouse flushes truly are. I had become spoiled on my first day. I thought that by the time I saw my tenth grouse that week I'd probably get one. Unfortunately, that would be my one and only shot all week.

Later that year I read a book by Dennis Walpole called

"The Grouse Hunter's Guide". I wish I had read it sooner because it gives you a great appreciation for how special grouse hunting can be. You have to have a good time grouse hunting even if you don't see a single bird for a week. It helps to set your perspective by knowing that you are seeking a very difficult game bird. I wasn't aware of that about grouse, at least not enough.

Another thing that helps you enjoy getting shut out hunting is camping with great people. The food and fun that happens around the campfire at night is often a better time than the actual hunting. And this trip was especially nice because there were so many Weimaraners running around.

My hunting skills were expanding on this trip. I now knew that grouse were fast, but at least the one I shot at flew in a straight line. Woodcock did not give me that same courtesy. These things swerved through the brush like bats. I feel no shame in saying I didn't hit a single woodcock all week. I could have stayed out there for a month with the same results. I don't know that I'll ever be able to hit something so small and quick. Fortunately, I travel with someone who is a better shot than me. Mary Ann shot one later in the week and let me help her eat it. Which was nice of her because woodcock are really only one bite big.

What I didn't get a sense of in hunting this thick brush was how Sadie and Grace were doing. They were not usually near me. I only saw flashes of them when they passed by. I could tell they were working hard but Mary Ann said the wild birds were flushing quicker than the preserve birds we were used to. Grace must have made the adjustment though because she pointed the woodcock that Mary Ann shot.

Needless to say, Sadie and Grace gave this trip a ten out of ten. Camp Weimaraner's liberal leash laws were a big hit. And there was bird hunting every day. There were other Weimaraner's to smell and plenty of belly rubs by the campfire.

As I said, this trip to Michigan was too much too fast for me. It was like the grouse that I missed. When something that good happens so quickly, you think there will be more opportunities just like it. But, life gets in the way and we haven't had the chance to get back out to Michigan or anywhere else that far since. With so much going on all the time, there's always something else to do. A long trip like that takes major planning and it hasn't happened yet. But, someday it will. I'm already planning out an alternate route around Pennsylvania.

Running for Office

Voting is our civic duty. So I go up to the school and vote every two years. I want to vote on important things like, "When does hunting season start?" or "How many geese can I shoot?" or "Can we get rid of speed limits?" But, I usually don't get to vote on those important things. The people that get to decide those things, or at least have some input on them, are elected officials. It was elected officials that decided to make it illegal to buy a gun on the Internet and have it shipped to my house. I can't figure out any good reason for this law. But, it made me think that it might be a good idea to watch these lawmakers more closely.

We have to pay attention to politics despite the fact that it's boring and we'd rather be out playing with Weimaraners. The people in the legislature, most of whom we didn't vote for, start trying to "help" us and we end up having to buy another sticker to put on something that we bought with our own money. But, it's not easy to find out what the politicians are up to. I watched an entire fifteen minutes of a county council meeting on cable TV. I endured this torture hoping to see them vote on something interesting. Instead, they talked about nothing the entire time. It was then that I realized two things. The interesting things happen away from the public eye, and I will never be able to stay awake long enough to hold public office. Still, I need to know what the government is doing.

Every time we need information these days we go to the Internet first. But, the Internet is a big letdown in this case. Maryland has a terrible website. However, it keeps the government from having to talk to people so if that's the goal, it serves its purpose. I find the site impossible to use. I dread the endless searches that find zero results. They provide the information they want to provide and I am supposed to be happy with that. It's rarely helpful. And it probably cost a billion dollars. I checked the F.A.Q. but "Why is your site so terrible?" isn't in there.

So, how do you get information about what's going on? Television is useless for getting information about what's happening in your neighborhood. Maryland television stations are in Baltimore, so they spend most of their time covering crime. The main newspaper in Baltimore is called the BS for a reason. It becomes less relevant every year. Radio is a good source of information, but I only listen to it when I'm driving. The unfortunate truth is that you have to spend time gathering your own information. You have to talk to people, keep your eyes open, get out of the house, go to local events that you aren't necessarily interested in, and always be on the lookout for potential allies. You can be sure there are groups of people that think like you do and want the government to stop meddling where it isn't needed.

A recent example of this government meddling concerns dog owners. The Maryland Legislature has been considering new dog laws that would ban pit bulls and punish their owners. Here we have a bunch of people that got elected without ever having their dog credentials questioned, deciding an issue for all of us. Never mind that pit bulls don't need to be banned. Once the legislature starts having a conversation about banning dogs, or anything else, it's a matter of time before they do something. Since they always go overboard in the name of public safety, I know they won't stop at pit bulls. All dogs will soon enter the conversation and be fair game for a government ban.

The unreliability of elected officials is a problem. I can't figure out what the Maryland state legislature is doing half the time. I took a look at the people in there and I see why things get so messed up around here. You never know what these people are going to do. They definitely can't be counted on to support dog issues correctly.

I've been forced to develop a plan that puts a Weimaraner in the state legislature, or at least on the county council. I need someone on the inside to protect my interests. It's the only way to get a consistently reliable dog vote. I know what people will say, "That's crazy", or "There are rules against that kind of thing". Well, rules about elections get bent and winked at all the time. My team and I are confident that we can get one of our dogs elected without anyone ever knowing she's a dog. It's unprecedented, but it's not like we're starting out trying to get elected president. We're starting out with a small office where often the people elected are never seen by citizens. Does anyone know their county council by sight? Not around here they don't.

Are we duping the public? Well sure, a little bit. But, that goes on all the time and no one makes a big deal out of it. In the great tradition of our two major political parties, we're "not providing more information than is necessary".

Election politics are different than the normal, "keeping track of what's happening" kind of politics. You have to have a strategy. One that plays to our candidate's strengths and assures us of victory. We have two Weimaraner's to choose from, both of whom bring certain things to the table.

We first considered Grace as our candidate. She's bright and outgoing. Always start with a candidate that's bright. She has a commanding presence with great instincts in a crisis. She doesn't lose her composure, she'll let you know who is in charge. But, she already thinks she's the empress of all she survey's. She seems unwilling to campaign for something as small potatoes as county councilman. And forget about debates, you can't win if you try to push your opponent off the stage while yelling "Off with your head!"

Unless we could figure out a way to work bird hunting into the daily grind of running for office, Grace is not going to stay as focused as we need her to be. Outdoorsmen would vote for her in droves but there just aren't enough of those droves. Grace wouldn't be interested in anything less than a federal level office anyway. She has always said, "If you are going to run for office anyway, get one that gives you some real power." We're going to keep Grace in reserve for now. If we ever get ready for the big time we might bring her in.

So, that leaves us with Sadie. She already has a bunch of qualities that I'd like to see in a politician. Sadie doesn't say much, she doesn't give speeches, she doesn't do fund raisers. We're lucky she has such a natural love for people, I've never seen anyone that doesn't like her. That's half the battle in politics. And it doesn't hurt that she's the most honest politician I've ever seen.

Sadie polls well in the crucial demographics. Young and elderly voters seem to be crucial to any election. These are Sadie's people. She has great strength in these voting blocs. College kids seem willing to follow any crazy idea so electing Sadie will only be natural to them. And they'll love a politician that sponsors "killer drink specials".

We're not going to overwhelm the voter with a lot of information. It's a mistake to take strong positions on issues.

Sadie's position on the issues is the same as all the voters because she's honest. Leave the specifics up to the voter's imagination. Who knows how many elections have been lost because the candidate did too much talking. She's going to work hard for her constituents, that's all they need to know.

We're planning an elaborate giveaway program. Voter turnout is crucial and people turn out best for free stuff. Why wait to be elected to start handing out the goodies to those that will return us to office time after time. Most politicians deal in pork, well Sadie deals in pork sandwiches. Free barbecue at every event is what people want. And Sadie can work a crowd. You haven't seen a politician turn on the charm the way Sadie can.

Sadie is corruption free. That's important and rare these days. She doesn't even know what money is. There are no skeletons in her closet, other than being a dog. And we plan to be vague on the whole dog issue. We've got all our press releases planned out. "Our opponent refuses to stick to the issues." "These dog questions are a distraction to keep people from examining our opponent's record." If her opponent tries to smear her with more accusations of being a dog, we'll respond with suitable outrage. "These accusations are preposterous." "The people of this county deserve better."

If they dare try showing pictures of Sadie being a dog we'll remind people that pictures can be altered, everyone has photoshop. There's no evidence so strong that it can't be refuted.

The candidate herself will remain above all this of course. The dignity of the office demands decorum. She's a serious candidate that takes this job seriously. Mudslinging is for childish, desperate losers.

People are always talking about the swing vote. We need them to swing our way. These people seem to be the ones that don't decide who to vote for until the last day. All that's needed to get these people to vote for us is a catchy jingle. We'll play it on the TV, radio, and Internet. We'll saturate the airwaves. Get something in people's head and they'll be humming it in the voting booth.

The ability to create an image seems to be the real power of the media. Politicians say a lot when they are running for office. And they say different things once they are in office. And people know that. That's why most people don't pay attention to what politicians say. It's the image that we end up voting for. The time for Sadie's silent campaign has arrived.

It's not like dogs aren't involved in the election process. It seems like every election cycle we see a report of someone's dog registering to vote. Of course we only see the stories of the ones that didn't make it. Does anyone really think every dog got caught before casting a vote? How many got through? Those poll workers are volunteers, you can't expect them to catch every dog that's trying to bluff their way past.

I've looked it up and found no historical record of Weimaraner's participating in electoral politics. Eisenhower's dog doesn't count. It's not surprising, considering their secretive origins, these dogs don't have a problem keeping their yapper shut. I wouldn't expect to see any overt admission of someone trying to get a Weimaraner elected to office anyhow. There was a time you might get into real trouble for something like that. Then again, fixing elections has a pretty long tradition itself. The point is, there seems to be more shady things going on during elections now than ever, with less consequences for the offenders. American politics are truly at a unique point.

Of course, I haven't forgotten that it costs money to get the public's attention. I read that each presidential campaign will be spending hundreds of millions of dollars. Imagine spending that much money and losing. They are spending way too much money for what they are trying to accomplish. I've been told the majority of that money is spent on ads and the rest on alcohol. If that's true, they seem to have the right approach, media image and giveaways. But, they don't have a good grasp of how to use money efficiently. And they still talk too much. One of their campaign promises should be to zip their lip once in a while.

We're out to prove that you can get elected on a budget.

This should be easy enough for an entry level job like county councilman. Estimates for the county council job are a few grand at most. I've appointed myself campaign manager in charge of Internet loot. I'm going to sell a whole bunch of stuff/junk on the Internet to fund this whole enterprise.

You may be thinking that I have spilled the beans here and now people will know what Sadie is up to. But, don't worry, it's likely no one will read this. If this book ever does see the light of day, the election will be long over and our success or failure will be history.

Nebraska

I flew out to Nebraska to meet Mary Ann and the pooches for a long weekend of sightseeing and no sleep. I'd been to Nebraska before so I'd seen most of it already. There's an overwhelming amount of corn and bean fields there so it's easy to get the idea that there's nothing else to see. It's a highly underrated state in the vacation fun category.

My advanced scout Mary Ann will find fun stuff to do no matter where we are. I knew she had probably planned more events than we would have the time or energy to do. She usually discovers things that the people living there didn't know about. And I've learned to stay flexible with my sleep requirements. The first rule of our vacations is to have fun. If we need more time for fun we'll trim it from the sleep schedule.

I got into Omaha very late, they were closing the airport when I arrived. We could have stayed at a hotel in Omaha but the plan said we had to drive an hour or so to where the fun was. By the time we got to where we were staying I was pretty much out on my feet. I hit the sack looking forward to five or six hours of sleep.

I woke up in a caboose in a Nebraska state park. This was cool because I'd never slept in a caboose. This was one of a number of train themed fun stops we'd be making. Trains are very prominent in Nebraska. Really, they have more trains than anywhere I've ever been.

I couldn't tell you how we got to the state park. And I couldn't tell you its name. I rarely know where I am when we are traveling. "Somewhere in Nebraska" is good enough for me. GPS and google maps are great if you are lost or can't find a good place to eat but I'm not usually interested in my exact location.

For our first activity of the new day we had to drive four hours so we could float down a river in a metal cattle feed tank.

I was aware of kayaking, canoeing, and tubing. But, tanking was a new one on me and I had agreed to give it a try. Tanking is the more communal version of tubing. Everyone is in the tank together so if it sinks you all go down together.

In the planning stages of this trip I had seen a brochure that raved about the great fun of tanking. I may have said something like "Sure let's give it a try." because it seemed so far away and unlikely to happen. But, I clearly remember that my first reaction was that I don't want to go. I have a legendary aversion to drowning. I've talked my way out of fifty or so white water rafting trips in my lifetime and expect to continue doing so forever. My fears were unwarranted in regards to tanking though. It's nearly safe, or at least as safe as it can be without lifeboats.

Tanking is closely related to tubing because in both of these sports you float down the river in a vehicle over which you have very little control. You don't care about this though because the first rule of tanking is enjoy your time on the river. Steering just gets you down the river quicker and that breaks the first rule of tanking.

By the time we arrived at the tanking/motor lodge there in the middle of Nebraska I had convinced myself that I would be the first ever tanking casualty. I was cursing the liars that made that brochure. I'd been deceived by doctored pictures of a pastoral scene with happy people on a calm shallow river. I wondered to myself how I had gotten suckered into this death float. I knew there would be rapids and I pictured myself trapped under a capsized tank.

Of course I got control of myself, opened the cooler, and was soon excited again about a day out on the river in some great weather. We were about to do something we'd never done before. I realized that I don't know anyone that's been tanking. I was a trailblazer, an adventurer, a person that did unusual things.

I was now anxious to get out on the river but I knew there'd be all kinds of red tape and rigamarole to go through before we got to the fun part. Much to my surprise there was no orientation class, no short safety film, no demonstration on life vest safety procedures, and most importantly no speeches about following the rules. (I ended up using my life vest as a seat cushion.)

We knew literally nothing about tanking so it seemed crazy to set us loose with expensive equipment on a wild river. Maybe "expensive" is stretching things a bit. Let's just say there was equipment. Still, some procedures on how to use this tank seemed to be in order.

What would we do in case of a tanking emergency? No idea. Apparently, there's never been one. But, I was thinking like I was still in Maryland. It's easy to forget that there are places that trust you to be responsible and don't try to control every aspect of your life.

There are no rules to distract you from the fun of tanking in Nebraska. At least, no one showed us any. When we said we had two Weimaraner's that wanted to go tanking with us I expected the usual "no dogs allowed" routine. Or at least some kind of hard time and maybe even an extra fee. But, the tanking officer in charge just said, "Whatever". Almost like she expected Weimaraner's to have more sense than that but the point is she didn't put up a fight about it.

There was only one paper to sign and we signed that sucker in two seconds flat. I didn't even read it. I didn't know if Mary Ann did or not. When we are on vacation, you don't put a piece of paper between us and fun. (For the record the paper said: If you get hurt tanking, we don't know you.)

We took the SUV to the finishing point and left it there. Then we boarded an old short yellow school bus for the ride back upriver to the starting point. This bus had seen better days and it was wheezing, squeaking, grinding, and just generally struggling to reach the posted speed. (30 mph) Just as I thought "At least we're on good paved roads." we turned off and were four wheeling it cross country. We were bouncing down the road/path and I began to sense some trepidation in our group. There wasn't much talking, not that we could hear each other over the bus engine, brakes, and squeaky seats. I thought maybe everyone was saying a silent prayer that we wouldn't get lost out here in the sticks and that the bus would make it to the starting point. I know I was. Sadie and Grace sensed something good was about to happen. They both perk up when we turn onto dirt roads because it usually means there's birds in the near future. Sadie is especially attuned to this. As soon as we go from dirt roads to asphalt she takes an immediate nap. I should have taken my cue from them and relaxed. We weren't really in the sticks anyway, we were in the Sand Hills. We couldn't have been more than a few hundred miles from civilization. Still, I sent my sister a quick text that I was somewhere in western Nebraska so she would know where to start looking if I didn't make it back.

The Sand Hills of Nebraska are much different than what I had seen in the eastern part of the state. They don't grow much corn out here at all. Probably because the land is too sandy. They don't have many sand dunes either so don't get the wrong idea. The Sand Hills have grass growing on them. Nebraska has a much more diverse terrain than most people think. Many people on the east coast think Nebraska is completely flat. But, it isn't.

The scenery on our grand tank tour was great. The land near the river was much greener than what we'd driven through that morning. It was just another example of Nebraska's surprising beauty. But, I reminded myself that it was summertime. In the winter I'm told it's a vast wasteland with high winds and snow drifts over your head most of the time.

We still had no idea how to tank but no one was giving out instructions so we shoved off and jumped in. They supplied us with paddles for some reason. For the most part we used the paddles to send the tank spinning out of control. Not that it was ever under control in the first place. Early in the voyage I used the paddle as a rudder and briefly stopped our spin. This fooled me into thinking I had some tank skills and so I did much more paddling than I should have. I soon realized my paddle was mostly for decoration and worked better if turned it around and used it as a pole to push off shallow spots.

Our tank had no captain and none of us had any experience, or interest, in commanding a sea vessel. Sensing this vacuum of power, Grace took charge. Weim Rule 57 states, "Grace is in charge until such time as she doesn't want to be in charge any more." Grace's easy confidence in her nautical abilities soothed the crews nerves and the early part of the journey passed without incident. She's a hands off kind of captain that doesn't say much and has liberal alcohol rules. Tough but fair, is how most people describe her.

The tank began to run aground repeatedly and the crew began to bicker. Grace blamed our inexperience and cried out for a steering wheel. Not for the first time I questioned the wisdom of getting into a feed tank. During one of these brief "Hey we're stuck again." incidents, Grace yelled land ho and jumped overboard. A more seasoned captain would have had us secure the tank first so that she would have a chance of getting back in, but not this one. She left those petty details to her crew. It showed a lot of confidence in us which we really appreciated. Once we had the tank beached up on a sandbar we awaited the return of our captain. Grace returned to the tank having claimed this land as her own. The territory formerly known as "Nebraska" was re-named Graceland. She's done this before and actually owns quite a bit of land, for a dog.

This was a wonderful spot on the river. Grace had chosen well. Much of the river that we saw went through a valley with steep (for Nebraska) ridges close to the shoreline. Here though there was a large field that stretched out on one side of the riverbank. The water was very shallow so we had lunch and declared a fifteen minute Weimaraner free for all. The grass was high, higher than a Weimaraner. So, we couldn't actually see them when they went ashore. There must have been some cool stuff in there though because every minute or so they would come crashing out of the grass and try to get us to follow them in. We weren't up for hiking though and finally convinced them to just play in the water. The weather was still holding out for us. It was very hot but there were enough clouds floating past to keep us cool. Sadie and Grace used this time for a general frolic and they even found one spot where they could swim against the current, a favorite Weimaraner pastime. Watching these two happily wear themselves out was a beautiful sight to behold because I knew they would sleep well that night. When the Weimaraner's sleep well, we all sleep well. These dogs have enough daily energy to light a small town. I wasn't sure this river was big enough to dissipate it. But, it definitely took the edge off them and we benefitted with some good quiet time later.

While I had had some nervousness about this tanking trip,

now I was dreading the end of it. Every bend in the river that wasn't the end of our trip was followed by a sigh of relief. I was just getting the hang of tanking but I knew that around one of these turns I'd see the SUV and the tanking adventure would be over. Eventually I was right. Grace gave us permission to go ashore. Staying consistent with tanking etiquette, there was absolutely no one at the finish line to debrief us or sell us commemorative shirts. We didn't even get a goodbye letter from a lawyer.

I don't know who first came up with the idea of floating down the river in a feed tank. There are a number of possible scenarios and most of them involve alcohol. One of them involves an adventurous cow enjoying a day on the river. It probably happened by accident but however tanking was discovered, you have to admire the entrepreneurial spirit that made someone realize they could make money off it. That kind of spirit is what made this country great.

We had a few great hours on the river. Being out in the some country that is still relatively undisturbed by civilization is a great experience. I always feel like I've gotten closer to really living when I do that.

I would recommend tanking to anyone. Especially people that swim like a stone, like me. I'm almost positive that I was never in any real danger of drowning in a two and a half foot river.

One of the things I liked best about this whole tanking deal was the feeling that we were getting away with something. It was a breath of fresh air for someone that lives in Maryland, where you can see evidence of government intrusion everywhere you look. Tanking was some non government regulated fun and that is the best kind to me.

We all piled back into the SUV and rolled on to our next stop. I had heard about a place called Carhenge. The pictures showed a bunch of cars stuck in the ground nose first and arranged in the shape of Stonehenge. We would never be closer than we were then so we made the trip. The brochure doesn't lie. It's a bunch of cars stuck in the ground and arranged in the shape of Stonehenge. No dogs were allowed but one of ours escaped and took the tour. Our luck was still holding out, we were the only ones visiting at the time and a little off the leash time for Sadie was no problem. Grace was passed out in the SUV. She was an exhausted former tank captain.

Carhenge is something to see if you are out that way. Although why you would be out that way I don't know. The main question about Carhenge is why someone would take the time to do it. It's an elaborate project with no obvious point. This is the same question I've always had about Stonehenge. There must have been arguments during the construction of Stonehenge. You know the people moving those big rocks started thinking, "Why are we doing this?", and "This is a lot of work for some kind of astrological clock that only works once a year." So, if you think you want to see Stonehenge, go see Carhenge first. It's just as good and the trip is shorter.

From Carhenge we headed to Scott's Bluff for some dinner and well earned sleep. I had a steak in Scott's Bluff that must have been great because I still remember it. It had so many mushrooms piled on it I had to drill for ten minutes just to hit steak. I generally don't remember my steaks for very long but this one was special. It had star power. The whole day had been memorable and I slept like a rock that night.

We left Scott's Bluff early the next morning, eager to say goodbye to a "janitorially challenged" hotel. I'm not saying the carpet in our room was old but it looked like it was left over from pioneer days.

We had been forced to make some hotel compromises while visiting Nebraska because most of the nicer, and unenlightened, places don't allow dogs. Last night's hotel, a major chain who's name I would love to tell you, was less than we had hoped it would be.

By the way, places that don't allow dogs are just begging for me to smuggle a couple of Weimaraner's in under my coat. I haven't done it yet, but it will happen. It's inevitable that eventually our options will be so few we won't have a choice. Hopefully there will just be a fine and some harsh words. I have always thought that if the managers of these snobby establishments could only meet our dogs then they'd see how cool they are and change their minds. Policies are made to be broken. There should be some kind of appeal process at least. Maybe a Weimaraner meet and greet. As far as I know, Sadie and Grace have never met any of these anti-dog hotel people. That's too bad because when these dogs lay on the charm there's no denying them anything.

We were headed for another big day of mid-west sight-seeing and it was going to have to be good to measure up to yesterday's sights.

Driving directly west out of Scott's Bluff we soon entered Wyoming. This being one of the few states I've never been to, I mentally checked it off the list. It's surprising to me how almost everyone keeps a mental list of states they've visited. Now that there are only a few left for me it takes a long time between checks. I'm over making special trips just to say I visited a particular state though. I once was ten minutes from Indiana and decided to turn back the other way. I'd like to be able to say I've visited every state eventually but I doubt it will happen. I only visit places that give me a reason to do so. I'm going to need a real good reason to visit states like Oregon and Washington. They are just too far away.

Our first stop today was the Guernsey Ruts. As usual my first reaction was to say "Ruts? We're visiting ruts?" Mary Ann said not to worry, I would like it. And I did.

At this location the rocky terrain forced nearly all the pioneer wagons on the Oregon-California trail to go through the same spot near the North Platte River. The ruts are five feet deep in some places and cut right into the sandstone. It's a reminder of just how many thousands of these wagons made the five to six month journey west. That's many more than I had been aware of. It would have been a great place for the first pioneer wagon drive-thru.

There are a ton of details about the pioneers that aren't common knowledge. I got tired of saying "Oh, I didn't know that." by the end of the day. Here are a few of the pioneer facts that I learned during my travels. To pull their wagons, oxen were the animal of choice over horses. Even though the horses were faster, a pioneer would have to carry food for the horse in the wagon. That was heavy stuff and took up much valuable space. Oxen could eat the prairie grasses in many places so you just had to wait for them to eat in the morning then you could head west. Horses were a target for theft because they were fast and useful. It isn't easy to steal oxen because they are so slow that rustlers couldn't get away fast enough. Imagine jumping on the back of an ox and trying to get away from anyone. Not going to happen. Another advantage of oxen over horses was that, If things got tough, and they probably would, oxen taste better than horses.

Back in those times, the trail was littered with heavy items that the pioneers had thought they wanted but soon abandoned. Travel light was not just a saying for these people. It was really serious wisdom.

Water is very heavy and the pioneers generally could not carry enough to last the entire trip so they drank what was available along the way. In this area the water of the North Platte was not safe to drink. There's an old saying that goes "The North Platte, too thick to drink and too thin to plow." Cholera is a disease caused by drinking contaminated water. This is a big problem when all you have to drink is contaminated water. If someone in your party got sick there was not a lot that could be done for them. There were no doctors and very little medicine. Plus, it wasn't well understood that the water was the reason people were sick. So any treatment was a guess or some sort of traditional remedy.

People that drank tea were generally healthier, but no one knew why. Turns out it had nothing to do with the tea, it was because they boiled the water and killed most of the bacteria. I would have been in big trouble because I don't like tea.

I had always pictured people riding these wagons west but the truth is that the wagons were luggage. Most of the pioneers walked all the way to California. And you just know they had great shoes.

Weimaraner's are nowhere to be found in any of the pioneer exhibits or literature. This is fortunate because even though Weimaraner's like a morning run, they'd be riding in the wagons by lunch time.

Wyoming is a wide open state, just as I'd imagined. You really get a sense that it hasn't changed much at all since the pioneers rolled through. People from the east coast have a picture that the west is completely flat until you get to the Rockies. Nebraska proved to me that isn't true and Wyoming proved it again. Where we entered, the ridges on either side of the highway were a beautiful golden color with just a touch of green. It reminded me more of California wine country than what I had imagined Wyoming would look like.

We passed through Fort Laramie so quickly we almost missed it. This town is also a historical pioneer site but we weren't aware of how significant it is, so we only stopped for a quick picture. That was a missed opportunity.

It was a beautiful day for walking in some ruts, sunny with temperatures in the low 90's. We arrived at Guernsey State Park and had the place to ourselves. The ruts are a national historic site inside a state park that is itself a national historic site for other reasons. This is a very unusual situation I believe and I was glad to be there. Several times since I'd been visiting Nebraska I had the feeling of being somewhere special and I had it again here. That's how you know you picked the right spot for a vacation. The site had a lot of history but not much else, just a few markers and an outhouse. There was no gift shop so I figured we would not be there long.

When we are in any large area with no other people around, let's just say; the Weimaraners run free. This is a dangerous operation that I don't recommend because these places are open to the public. You never know when an inconvenient member of the public will show up and ruin your good time. The public is like that, always showing up unannounced.

For now though, this national historic site was declared Weimaranerland, and away they went. When they are first let off the leash, Sadie and Grace exude a joy so great I wish I could experience it. But, not enough to put the leash on.

Even in a park of this size we are sure to clean up the dog poop. And I have to say it feels more than a little odd to pick up some poop in the middle of a thousand acre field. We are soooo civilized.

As the dogs tore off I knew they would not behave as normal tourists do. They do not bother to read any signs and do not stay on the marked paths. Then I noticed that there were no signs or barriers to keep people and their dogs off the ruts. It could be that Wyoming is run by people that aren't obsessed with controlling the public. It was my second experience with this in two days and I hoped it would continue. If this park was in Maryland there would probably have been electrified fence and overpaid guards.

Grace is very focused when she gets a scent in her nose. She runs with a sense of purpose that excludes petty things like self preservation and she always has her nose to the ground. That's why I wasn't surprised when she emerged from the underbrush with a cactus stuck to her nose. She impatiently allowed me to pull the majority of it off but I could see spines still stuck in her nose. We'd be spending some time later getting them out back at the SUV. Meanwhile, she had a brand new state park to smell and couldn't waste more time with me.

As I walked around the area I thought the pioneers could have done worse than settling down right here in this spot. The ground is kind of dry and rocky and there were Weimaraner's running everywhere but to my twenty first century eye it was great. I suppose the pioneers weren't impressed by wide open spaces and great views. They were really focused on finding a better life in California. I really hope they were successful but at this point in time, Wyoming is the better spot.

For the twentieth time that weekend I was amazed by the

pioneers sheer determination in undertaking a journey that killed many of them. I don't really understand why so many of them decided to go west. I know the reasons that many of the women wrote in their journals but I can't quite believe them. It seems that you would have to be naive to believe the claims that were made about life in California. And if there's one thing the pioneers were not, it's naive. I also don't think the places they left were all that bad. They weren't exactly fleeing from Venezuela or Iran. They left places like Ohio and Illinois. Not terrible places to live by many standards.

We spent close to an hour at the ruts. That seemed like plenty of time to get the whole experience because really they are just ruts. As I was heading down the hill back to the SUV Grace skidded to a stop in front of me and limped once before running off. At that exact moment Mary Ann yelled from up the hill to check the dogs out because she saw some blood drops on the sidewalk. Sadie was standing still so I suspected she might have a foot issue. I grabbed her and gave her the once over. She was covered in historical pioneer dust but she had no injuries.

I called Grace back and she stood impatiently while I did my inspection. She still had the cactus thorns in her nose and now she had torn the big pad on her front right paw almost completely off. Disappointment covered her face as we ruled her day at the ruts was over.

Once we got her to the SUV we went to work on the cactus spines first. She is a relatively good patient compared to some dogs I know. Grace doesn't whine or shy away from something painful. She seems almost too proud to admit that she ever feels pain. It seems that she does trust us but it's an impatient kind of trust. She fidgets like a kid whose parents are embarrassing her by making a fuss in front of her friends. Getting those spines out had to hurt but she took it well. Some of them were less than half an inch long and hard to grab.

Moving to the more serious injury, the patient was willing to trade a belly rub for a close inspection of her paw. I had never seen a pad almost torn off like this. And I've never seen a dog less concerned about it. If we had rubbed a little dirt on it and told her to get back out there she would have been gone in a flash. If I had this much skin ripped off of me they would have been calling an ambulance because I'd have been on the ground refusing to move.

There was very little blood, just some clear fluid that I can never remember the name of. I remember thinking of course there's no blood there because there's no nerves there. As I looked at Grace's paw I realized the pad is just a big callous that they build up on their feet. Don't ever say I can't grasp the obvious.

Mary Ann has some great first aid kits for dogs and

people. I really hope we never need half the stuff she carries in them. We got the dust washed off her paw and bandaged the flap up like a blister, hoping it would magically re-attach. Then we taped a sock on her foot until we could get back to the hotel to get the orange hunting shoe that maybe she should have been wearing in the first place. Although, I hesitate to say that, the terrain was dry but no tougher than many places we've hunted with no problems. The major problem is that Grace doesn't cut her pads any breaks. She demands performance from them. She stops running by skidding like a cartoon dog and that is probably what happened to her pad. I've seen her stop like an ice skater on a concrete sidewalk. I suspect this is far from the last time we will be wrapping up one of her feet.

After declaring her fit to travel we loaded up the SUV and headed out of Wyoming with some great memories and only one slightly injured dog. We still had more sights to see and many miles to travel before we would sleep. On the ride out of Wyoming we realized that Grace needed to take it easy for a few days to let her foot heal. Then we realized this would get an immediate veto. She just isn't going to take it easy without the use of force. She shrugs off threats and ignores the advice of her doctors with reckless abandon. It would be like telling a young child they had to go back to the hotel after spending a half day at Disney World. They might do it but you'll hear about it. And every place we go seems like Disney World to Grace.

There would be no saving the pad however. We ended up cutting the flap of pad off later that night. I remembered the next day a story about Stevie Ray Vaughn gluing calluses back onto his hand so he could continue playing guitar. I don't know if it would have worked or not but I know Grace would have been up for trying it.

Wyoming is a big state and you might say it wasn't fair for it to gang up on one little dog. However, Grace isn't afraid of Wyoming one bit so don't feel sorry for her. Wyoming scored a tiny victory against Grace today, but this state doesn't realize that our dog has a long memory. When she returns to Wyoming, and she will, she'll be looking to settle the score.

True History of the Weimaraner

When I realized that Weimaraner's were going to be my favorite breed of dog, I wanted to learn as much about them as possible. By now I've read quite a few short histories, and two long ones, about this dog. If the long histories are correct then many of the short ones are wrong. The main trouble with these short history lessons is that they play down the fact that there's very little undisputed knowledge. If you repeat some speculation enough times it starts to gain real credibility. That's the Internet effect.

The are a number of factors that led to our lack of information about the Weimaraner. The sum total of these factors force us to conclude that the Weimaraner is a dog with dark and mysterious origins that have been lost in time. At least it is fun to say that to Sadie and Grace. They seem to like being dark and mysterious.

If you have paper records that you don't want to lose, don't store them in pre World War I Germany. The city of Weimar seems to have been the location where a significant amount of Weimaraner development occurred. Bombs aren't good for most filing systems, no matter how organized. Weimar didn't fare well in either World War and any paper records were probably lost. But, if you've ever seen breeding records you know how boring they can be so it doesn't seem worthwhile to dwell on their loss.

Also, the men that developed the Weimaraner had no intention of telling the general public anything about it. They were extremely secretive about the Weimaraner and kept the numbers down below fifteen hundred. The German Weimaraner Club was started in 1897. Only members of the club were permitted to own Weimaraner's and I doubt it was easy to get a membership card. So, even if there are records somewhere, these guys aren't talking.

Even though we may never know the details of the Weimaraner origins, it's fun to speculate. William Denlinger documents some of the theories that were in existence at the time his book was written. We'll go through them later if you would like.

Right now I would like to present the first true and complete history of the Weimaraner. The previous unsuccessful histories have tried to use facts and evidence to give a picture of the development of the Weimaraner. Anyone that lives with one will tell you that Weimaraner's don't care about facts or evidence. (Unless the facts are sitting on the kitchen counter in a takeout box.)

Weimaraner's are complex characters that must have had an equally complex development plan. Perhaps the plan worked too well. Maybe these dogs weren't supposed to be this way.

The true history of the Weimaraner is more than just birth records and old German guys on horses. If you dispute any of my findings it may be that you know too much about breeding dogs. I am not limited by any such knowledge. Using nothing but the power of observation and deductive reasoning skills I've put together the missing pieces.

Weimaraner's have all the versatile gun dog characteristics that they need to be successful in the field. They have good seeking, pointing and retrieving ability, they work well in (warm) water, and they are steady around guns. They even listen well when they want to.

In addition to all these normal hunting dog traits, Weimaraner's have other talents that you won't see listed in any book. However, their owners are well aware of many of them. Many of these talents don't seem to have clear functions yet. They are probably for future use.

If you've been able to keep your Weimaraner's out of your bed, you have my congratulations. If you haven't then you know Weims can flow like water across the entire bed. If I sit up in bed for some reason, to check the time or re-arrange pillows, both dogs will often flow right into my spot. Turn the light on to see what happened and you'll see them both still asleep and completely unaware that this has happened, their little halo's sparkling in the moonlight. Just the other day

I saw Sadie swim across the bed with her back legs straight out behind her. She got to the edge and just kept right on going. The illusion that she was in water was amazing. Mary Ann calls that Sadie's favorite dismount. It's a true miracle that in only one hundred years of dog breeding, Weimaraner's can take the shape of their container. Which means they have a higher water content than other dogs, maybe 80-90 percent. I'm not sure what use it could possibly serve in hunting birds but the ability is there. Maybe this is what hunter's mean when they refer to "a good water dog". We have to just trust the German's on this one.

Everyone knows that Elephants never forget anything. Don't ask me how they did it, but this steel trap memory trait was built into the Weimaraner. They never forget anything either. One day in the field we noticed Sadie paying a little too much attention to a particular spot. For some reason these dogs never find anything in the field that smells good and won't hurt them. It's always the smelly, dangerous stuff that is most interesting. Not wanting to have to hose off whatever it was later, we ran her off it. But, it was too late. Her nose had the coordinates. She left it but unknown to us she filed away that stinky spot for later use. We got in the truck and drove to the Arctic Circle. For three months we hunted polar bears and lived on nothing but whale blubber. Then we drove back home, let Sadie out of the truck, and she made a beeline for that same spot in the field. It was a total elephant moment and it was then that I realized Weimaraner's are part elephant. Their memory is attached to their nose. But, it's not like the way our nose is attached to our memory. Human's smell something and are reminded of times we smelled it before. Once a smell gets in that Weimaraner's moosh it is trapped forever, available for sampling. It's like a nose hard drive. Or a hard nosedrive.

We find ourselves walking along trails with the Weimaraner's quite often. Sadie will trot along until something pings per radar, then she suddenly freezes and switches to slow motion stalk mode. Then she steps very slowly and gingerly like she's sneaking up on something. She stays in this mode until her prey sees her and runs off. But, it's not just an outdoor technique. Sadie's employs this same mode indoors to sneak up on balls or chew toys, especially if I am holding it. I'm not sure if she is pretending to be invisible or just thinks she is that stealthy. Sometimes she'll stalk the toy to within a few inches before she strikes.

We were watching one of those wildlife shows and I noticed that cheetah's do the same thing. They creep up on their prey, slowly stepping through the tall grass. Then they strike. It's too similar to be a coincidence. So clearly, Sadie has cheetah blood in her veins. She's a fast runner but not as fast as a cheetah. She's got the slow, stalking cheetah blood in her, not the sixty mile an hour blood.

Needless to say, the way they swim, Weimaraner's have been crossed with some kind of fish. They don't just love the water, they loooooove the water. The question is, which kind of fish did the Weimaraner developers use? There are a lot different kinds of fish to choose from. Then I noticed that fish seem bored by water. They are so over water. Fish notice water about as much as we notice air. We only think of it when we can't get enough.

This kind of bored fish attitude doesn't resemble the Weimaraner approach to water at all. So, what kind of water loving swimmer were Weimaraner's crossed with? These dogs are glad when they see some water and it shows. Just walk up to the edge of a pond or lake and their tails will start shaking and Sadie will give you that look, "I'm going in the water Ken." Sadie swims with great enthusiasm and Grace swims to keep an eye on Sadie. We can barely keep Sadie out of the water and Grace will follow her anywhere. Sadie would jump into a pool of lava to retrieve a stick and Grace would go in right behind her to take the stick back. I swim like a rock so it's amazing to me how well dogs swim with no training. Sadie and Grace swim and still follow directions. I don't multi-task in water, it's all about survival for me. Like George Carlin said, swimming isn't a sport, it's a way to keep from drowning. There's no panic in Sadie though, she's as comfortable in water as she is on the couch.

It's not all fun and games for her though, retrieving sticks in the water is serious business. If Sadie swims out into the water and can't find the stick, she'll look back to the shore for more detailed instructions. She'll give you the "little help" look and then go wherever you point her to go. That's a dog that's having fun in the water, not worrying about drowning at any moment like I usually am. Unconcerned for her safety, and loving every minute in the water, that's Sadie.

Then I realized that Sadie and Grace aren't part fish at all, they're part dolphin. Dolphins love to swim and it shows. They seem to have the same enthusiasm as these Weimaraner's. I've stood on the shore at Ocean City many times and watched dolphins swim by. It can't be a matter of survival to swim real fast and pop out of the water periodically. I know they have to breathe but it seems like they are having a lot of fun doing it too. Dolphins do more swimming than is necessary. That's very unfishlike, but's it's not unWeimaranerlike. This relationship explains the love Weims get out of swimming, and the active blow hole.

For a while I thought Weimaraner's were crossed with a grey hound bus. They produce about the same amount of fumes and sometimes the exhaust can knock you off your feet.

Weimaraner's are definitely part alligator. If you've ever

seen one of those alligator death rolls on TV then you can imagine one of these dogs when they discover something stinky in the field. The difference is that Weimaraner's do a love roll instead of a death roll. The goal for Sadie and Grace seems to be to get as much coating on as possible. That way they might get to take some smell home with them. They know there's going to be a thorough hosing off, they just hope we'll miss a little bit.

Another animal secretly involved in the development of Weimaraner's are bears. Bears and people don't get along as well as Weimaraner's and people. And unfortunately there are a number of cases of bears attacking humans. While you do not see packs of man-eating Weimaraner's in the woods, there is a common trait between the two. Bears will eat anything and so will Weims. Most dogs have undiscriminating tastes, the world is their buffet. I don't know if Sadie and Grace ever regret having eaten things that smelled like food but were not. They are smart dogs so I wouldn't be surprised if, at least once in a while, they had eater's remorse and thought, "Next time I'll let her try it first."

Clearly, Weims can pay a price for this bearish dining style. I've seen Sadie lay around looking green after eating what she thought was a delicious lunch. She doesn't stay that way for long of course. She either keeps it down or tosses it back up and goes on about her day. All is forgotten in minutes. And

Grace is no slouch in the cast iron stomach department. She just recently ate a tube of delicious lip balm, kept down the good part, and yakked the tube back up. Now, that's talent.

Of course, dogs like Weims get bloat, or gastric torsion, which is when their stomach flips. And it is no joke. Usually this happens if they get strenuous exercise right after eating. But, as usual with the bad stuff you never know what might bring it on. I watched a first aid video where the vet has to reach in to untwist the stomach. Watching this video almost gave me the bloat. No thanks, I hope someone is working on breeding this particular trait out of Weimaraner's.

The difference between a bear's stomach and a Weim's is immense. What in the world is a bear's stomach made from anyway? Bears are omnivores; which means they are allowed to eat anything, unlike Weimaraner's, that only think they can. I have no idea if bears get upset stomachs, there should be some price to pay for standing in a river and eating fifty salmon. If they don't get upset stomachs then it is one of the great mysteries of the world.

When Weimaraner's get scared they shed more. This is very much like a skink, which sheds its tail when it gets scared. I've never seen a Weimaraner actually lose its tail due to being frightened but most of the ones I've seen do have short tails. They probably weren't all cut off by vets. And no one is going to tell you that their dog's tail just fell off when it got startled. The coincidence is too big to ignore and the Weimaraner being crossed with a skink is confirmed.

Previously, we had confirmed and then rejected the idea that Weimaraner's were part fish. Additional evidence was uncovered and we were forced to reconsider. This further research changed our very open minds. We discovered a trait that is indeed a true link to fish while watching Grace eat through a cow bone. The particular fish which Weimaraner's share a link is the deadly piranha. These fish are particularly aggressive, and effective in eating their prey. When the cow bone was examined by an objective third party, it was determined that the bone had been attacked by either a school of piranha or one crazed Weimaraner. This just goes to show that this kind of detailed genetic research is not easy to accomplish. And the science is never settled.

When we are in the truck Sadie is able to slither into the front seat like a snake. She knows that the front seat is for people and the back seat is for Weimaraners. But, that rule is one she never gets tired of trying to break. I don't know why she thinks this will work, she always gets caught. She's not nearly as sneaky as a snake. So she must be crossed with some kind of cute, goofy snake with a big moosh. She also likes to lay in the sun, just like her cold blooded relatives. Snakes have to sit in the sun to keep warm because they can't regulate their temperature. Sadie can regulate her temperature, she just likes it to be as high as possible. It's not unusual for her to walk into the house panting from an afternoon sunbath.

There's a little bit of weasel in every Weimaraner too. If Grace can get her nose into an area then she can get her whole body in there. I keep waiting for her to get stuck under a door. You may think there is no more room on the couch until Grace flops down and slowly sinks to the sofa like sand through the hourglass. There's never not enough room for Grace on a sofa. And just like a weasel, she likes pigeons and their eggs. Theoretically, Grace would never get a pigeon egg but somehow she is able get one every once in a while. I like my pigeon eggs cooked, usually scrambled or fried, Grace chomps them raw in one bite.

Weimaraner's are part Walmart greeter too. I didn't even know they had Walmart's in nineteenth century Germany but I can't deny the evidence. In fact, Weimaraner's would be the best greeters ever. Since they are actually happy to see you, their enthusiasm for the job would be infectious. They set a high bar in the greeting category. It's not a job to them, it's who they are. These two wiggle butts are so happy to see me when I get home that it really makes me feel good. (A "wiggle butt" is defined as a dog that wags it's tail so hard, the whole back end of the dog wiggles too.) And I don't have to be gone that long. If I go to the store for a few minutes it's like

I've been gone for days. It's joy that you just don't see from people. These dogs don't take for granted that you will come back. When I walk to the mailbox they can watch me the whole way. But, they're still crazy happy when I get back. Its like, "Hey it's Ken! Let's get him! We saw you over by the mailbox and we weren't sure you'd come back and then you did! Hey Ken, rub my belly!"

As much as Grace studies Sadie, you'd think she be more like her. But, Grace is her own dog with specific traits. Watch her eat one time and you'll know Grace is part cow. I think she only has one stomach but she chews like a cow. She's got that slow circular lower jawbone motion going. To make the image complete, sometimes she'll just stare at you while she's chewing like a cow does. If Grace isn't part cow then she's the most brilliant cow impersonator I've ever seen. Sadie doesn't do it and I haven't seen other dogs do it either. So Grace must come from a special cow breeding branch of Weimaraner's.

Grace also seems to be crossed with a venus fly trap. I've never seen Sadie do this either, but Grace snags flies right out of the air with ease. I guess she thinks they are really small birds. She's got quick jaws like a shark. It's both handy and gross at the same time. The first time I saw her do it, I couldn't quite believe what I had seen. It took a few more times before I was a believer. She knows this is quite a trick too and is not humble about it. She looks at you with a satisfied smirk on her face after each catch. I've thought about renting her out to make some extra cash. The world's only Weimaraner Fly Trap would be great at picnics and outdoor parties. But, I don't want her filling up on flies, her trips to the yard are adventurous enough as it is.

This review is incomplete. New abilities are discovered all the time. Weimaraner's are like a Swiss army knife dog with infinite attachments. Still, I hope this list gives you an idea of the special traits and extra functionality that have been built into the Weimaraner. Your own Weimaraner may include these traits and more, depending on the breeder. Remember, these dogs come equipped with the best in German engineering. Some of the things Weimaraner's can do don't have an obvious function yet, but the possibilities for the future are endless.

The Rare and Elusive Purple Weimaraner

I have a purple Weimaraner running around here that I'd like to enter into some dog events. I'm certain she could win some prizes if the AKC would just be reasonable.

The AKC is strict about the color of a Weimaraner's coat. Blue Weimaraner's are disqualified from AKC events. Even though they are beautiful dogs, the thinking is that they are not Weimaraner's, that they are cross bred with some other dog. Not everyone buys that argument of course. There is a group of blue Weimaraner owner's working to change this. I looked online to see if I could team up with this group but they don't need my help, they are way more organized than I.

It seems possible that the AKC and Weimaraner groups of other countries will one day recognize the blue Weimaraner. But, it will be a lot longer before the AKC includes purple Weimaraner's. Since I seem to have the only one, I doubt anyone is going listen to me. There's no association of purple Weimaraner owners for me to turn to. Nor can I locate another owner of this rare specimen.

In fact, I may be the co-owner of the only purple Weimaraner in existence. Although she is not strictly purple all the time. We don't show her to the AKC when she is in her purple color phase.

Right now Grace is sporting her late spring purple patina. It is gorgeous, at least in some spots. In others it still has seeds in it. There's two advantages to this kind of coat. One is that she's easy to spot in the field. The other is that it's made completely from delicious mulberries. Mulberries are similar to blackberries and have been known to stain nearly any material. I have heard that mulberries will stain teflon but have not confirmed it.

Grace starts with her basic shimmery gray coat. It's a blank canvas to her. She then creates her masterpiece by laying on her back like Michelangelo painting the Sistine Chapel. The only difference between her and Michelangelo is that Grace can take her art with her. She's a portable Weimaraner road show. She's the only dog you'll see carrying modern art on her back. And the berry art doesn't easily wash off. Once it dried it's almost like a mulberry tattoo.

There are a number of things Grace could be rolling in at the farm. And believe me, I'm happy when she chooses a berry bush. Mulberries are my preferred medium by far. Some of her "paints" are not nearly as nice to look at, or smell.

It is surprising that Grace would spend time wallowing in mulberries because as much as she likes them on her outside, she loves them on her inside. She's like a berry vacuum cleaner around the farm. She's got the technique refined so much that she can take the ripe berries off the bush and leave the unripe ones behind. It shows that she's not all about power and brute strength. She can use finesse when she has to. We might have to put the kibosh on this grazing though, or soon we'll be able to see a Grace browse line around all the berry bushes. Sadie likes berries too but seems to prefer that each one be handed to her individually. Apparently, this is why Sadie keeps us around. She doesn't like to get hit with the thorns. Grace eats the thorns.

To say it's a long shot that the AKC or WMA will ever recognize our rare breed of Weimaraner is being generous. They don't change the standard very often and I'm not much of a lobbyist. I'm keeping my eye on the blue Weimaraner group to see if they ever have any success in getting accepted. If the AKC budges on blue's then I might have a shot.

Dog shows exclude certain dogs from participating for a variety of reasons. They don't come right out and say, "Your dog is just too ugly to be seen by the general public." They cite the standard and say "We have to draw the line somewhere." But, the effect is the same.

We don't take Sadie and Grace to dog shows. And not because we've been told to keep our ugly mugs at home. The reason we choose not to participate is that there aren't enough areas to showcase our dog's strengths. What we need are some new categories. Our strongest category would be best tasting dog in show. I don't mean the judges should eat the dog, don't be gross. We have ensured that our dog has wallowed in only the finest organic mulberries, at the peak of flavor. The judges should eat that up. I've seen some dog shows but never once have I seen a judge taste a dog's coat. But, I've seen stranger stuff than that, so anything is possible.

Grace would do well in an artistic expression category as well. She has a lot to say, clearly, and she lets her art do the talking. She doesn't give autographs but if you are lucky you might get her personalized purple push.

Somehow she's able to achieve a delicate lavender mulberry veneer that will thrill the crowds if she ever gets to go public. How does she get it to look like that? I've seen her do it and I still don't know. It's a secret technique. She's worked with mulberries for most of her life. Some artists do it with paint, Grace does it with berries. Don't think that you can just let your dog roll in some berries and start calling it art. Most dogs can't get more than a rough purple smear effect. Leave it to the professionals.

Right now Grace has a nice interpretation of an impressionist seascape across her right ear. Up close it looks like a mess but from far away it's breathtaking. You just can't teach that kind of talent to a dog. They either have it or they don't. I don't like to throw around the word genius indiscriminately. But if it fits who am I to say otherwise?

If dog shows would expand their agenda's to include this

kind of performance art who knows what the results could bring. It opens up a whole range of possibilities. Maybe even people that didn't have dogs entered in the show would attend.

There are tons of things dogs can do that aren't covered by dog shows. It's all about looks at a dog show and honestly that train arrives at snoozeville early in the morning. Agility tests and field trials don't give us a comprehensive look at what dogs can do either. There should be real contests that people want to see. I'm not talking about made up contests like fastest scratcher, counter surfing, or competitive napping. I mean real demonstrations of dog talent.

An obvious place to start is the nose. Best nose in show should be a coveted prize. This is the most overlooked part of the Weimaraner. The standard says the nose should be gray. Really? That's it? That's a pretty low bar for something so important in the field. Finding birds is more of a nose activity than a visual activity. And dog show people would be smart to find a way to recognize the importance of the nose. Smell contests would be a big hit at shows. It would just take some creativity to come up with a way to judge them. Anyone can smell a pizza, a dog can probably tell you what kind of mushrooms are on it, from thirty feet away. When a dog correctly identifies the pizza box that contains shitake mushrooms out of ten other boxes you'll see standing ovations. When was the last time you saw that at a dog show? I can't believe no one has thought of this before.

Many people think the white spot on a Weimaraner's chest should be a minor fault. But, if the AKC is going to allow dogs with a white spot on their chest into the show, how about having some fun with it. By awarding a "best white spot in show" prize, dog shows could show how inclusive and friendly they are becoming. It's the new dog show attitude.

Sadie would not qualify for this particular prize as she has no white spot. But, Grace has a really cool one. It's in the shape of a star. It's rare to see one so cool. It is part of her fancy name, South Paws Blue Star Heaven Scent. Some people really don't like the white spot. But, no one seems to want to say that a small white spot should be disqualified. Getting a prize for a cool white spot would make people feel better about having it.

These are just some suggestions. The point is that dog shows have gotten stale. They need to widen their perspective if they want to keep the kids interested.

I know all this may never happen. It's probably a pipe dream. Grace's talent may never be recognized by the world. She may continue to toil in obscurity. Dog shows will probably never let rebel dog's like Grace reach their full capability. But, that's ok with us and she certainly couldn't care less. She's happy as long as she has berries to roll in. And many artistic geniuses weren't recognized in their own time.

The Breed is More Than Skin Deep

At the time that Sadie was growing from a puppy to a full grown Weimaraner, I began to be more interested in dog breeds. Sadie seemed different to me than other dogs I'd known. I didn't know if this difference had to do with her being a Weimaraner or if she was just one of a kind. I also really liked the way Sadie looked. Although, I knew she was more than just a good looking dog. She was inquisitive and loved to learn new things. But, I could see why people bought Weimaraners based on what they look like. I have to admit that I thought the "breed" of dog basically meant what the dog looked like. I knew somewhere in the back of my mind that it was more than that. But it was way in the back. I'd seen people with all sorts of different breeds of dog and never thought about the different challenges that they had to face based on their kind of dog.

This was the first time I noticed that many people have a favorite breed of dog. Just why that would be I didn't know. I started noticing dogs more and tried to identify each one that I saw. It became a challenge. Identifying dogs is kind of like identifying trees. Some are easy and some are not. The differences can be slight. I can pick out a German Shepard easily but I can't tell you which type of Shepard it is. I don't want to be that good at it.

Mutts are a particular problem when you are playing name that dog. Each dog is a walking quiz. I've seen dogs that don't appear to be any particular breed. Trying to identify mutts is fun but quickly becomes impossible. Some have such an elaborate family tree that they don't even appear in guidebooks. For these specimens I just conclude that if it barks, it's a dog.

Fortunately, my local area is crawling with dogs. This was an easy way to expand my knowledge. I went out and did an under cover dog study. I stayed under cover because people don't like to be studied. And they don't want anyone to know if they don't carry poop bags.

Of course, I saw lots of Labs. The word is out on Labs. They're great dogs. Labs are what Americans think of when they think of dogs. There are so many Labs around here that you would think they were giving them away.

This neighborhood has lots of other dogs too. People have put some thought into which kind of dog they want to own. They must see a difference, but again, I had thought the differences were superficial.

To get a comprehensive cross section of the dogs in my neighborhood, all I had to do was sit on a bench in the little park and watch them parade by, out for their morning stroll. What I saw was that each owner was attached to their breed of dog. They were as convinced about their breed as I was becoming about Sadie. Most of the dogs around here are a recognizable breed. There's very few mutts, not like when I was a kid.

I could see the attraction in nearly every type of dog. Only a few, which shall remain nameless, were completely out of the question for me. But here's a hint, the dogs I don't like are small dogs with bad attitudes. I like larger dogs, but I envy the fun size poop bags carried by tiny dog owners. (The dogs, not the owners.) I thought that I was getting pretty good at identifying the dog breeds around here when one day we were all driving along and passed a dog and its owner. I said to myself, "Lab". Mary Ann said, "That's a Golden." I replied, "Well they're almost the same." I'd seen so many Labs I became complacent. Rookie mistake but hey, no one's grading me right?

That's when Mary Ann said something about them not being the same at all. A light flickered on in my mind. I asked why she had decided on a Weimaraner. She had wanted a good versatile hunting dog with a no maintenance coat. What they looked like was irrelevant. I had never thought of it like that. Making such a logical choice, focused more on what kind of dog you were getting instead of how it looked was a great way to be sure you were happy with your dog. I don't know anyone else that chose their dog that way. The fact that

I don't know many hunting dog owner's might account for this.

My evaluation of dogdom wasn't going to be nearly so well thought out or logical. I'm an impulse buyer. I wait until I'm hungry to go to the grocery store. For my purposes I was strictly interested in how the neighborhood dogs looked. It didn't matter if they were easy or difficult to live with. I saw zero dogs that I liked as much as Sadie. Going on looks alone is a huge mistake. But, I figured I already had my dog, I just needed to make sure I liked it.

Sadie and I seem to match up well. She wants to chase the ball and I want to throw it. Although, she wants to chase the ball more than I could possibly throw it. Sadie isn't a low key dog. She's like a magnet for attention. People stop me on the street to ask about her. They yell at me at red lights. I didn't think I'd enjoy that much attention, but I do. Sadie makes me cooler just because I know her. Although I can say for certain that her coat is the only thing low maintenance about her, there's something about her that makes all her nonsense worth it. That's how I became certain that Weimaraner's were the dog for me. Weimaraners are my "go to" dog.

But, where were the other Weimaraners? If these dogs are so great, what's with all these other dogs? Whenever I buy a new car or truck I see a lot more of that model than I ever did before. I figured getting a Weimaraner would be similar, but it wasn't. When you have dogs you see more dogs, but I hardly ever see Weimaraners. I can count on one hand the Weimaraners I've seen around here. There was one in a car at the shopping center that had a pink collar. I'm guessing "female" because I'm like Sherlock Holmes. There was another Weimaraner out for a walk on the jogging path with it's owner. I saw this one a lot and called him Jack because I didn't know his real name. And finally there was one standing on the roof of a Toyota pick up at the gas station. He crawled out the back window and had a long rope tied somewhere inside the truck. That's it. In five years. And two of them could have been the same dog. This place is a Weimaraner desert.

I started wondering how people had begun keeping dogs in the first place. I was probably thinking too much at that time. Thinking too much usually leads to learning something I wish I didn't know. You'd think I'd learn not to think so much. One day I noticed Sadie trying to push me out of my chair. Usually she'll share, but not today. She wanted the entire chair. Without even thinking about it, I got up and moved to the couch. Then I thought, wait, what just happened there? She thinks that is her chair and I'd rather get up than fight her over it. It was then I realized that my relationship with Sadie was at least semi-complex. So, it was only natural that I began to think about how we'd gotten to that point.

I decided to start at the beginning. Dogs had to be the easiest animal to domesticate in the history of the world. The negotiations must have gone something like this. Dog: "Let me get this straight, you'll feed me, let me hang out by the fire in your cave and feed me. All I have to do is help you hunt for food everyday, herd a few sheep, and you'll keep me safe and feed me?" Man: "That's right." Dog: "I'm in."

It was clearly a match made in heaven because the relationship has endured for, I am told, thousands of years. But, that doesn't mean the relationship hasn't changed. Not many of us depend on our dog to help us put food on the table. And even fewer people have any sheep to herd. Not many people use dogs for security. Not really. I always think of the proverbial dog guarding the junk yard. That's good work if you can find it, but it's more rare all the time.

So, now that we've rid the dog of the few duties they had, why do we continue to keep them? Certainly the dogs aren't complaining. But, people seem happy to be forever stuck with dogs as well. The relationship has evolved but it continues long after the reasons that it started have faded away.

We had good reasons for starting our relationship with dogs. But, why continue to have dogs? We must get something out of it. Whatever it is, it's not a material benefit.

The vast majority of dog owners bought them to be family pets. They don't expect to get anything from the dog except maybe some good times.

Some of us are trying to preserve the hunting and herding skills of our dogs but our numbers are low. The average intelligence of people that hunt with their dog is clearly very high. And they are mostly better looking than other people too. There just aren't enough of us to make much difference. It's important to our traditions and it feels great to get your hunting dogs out in the field. But, again, can we make the argument that we need these dogs? That we can't live without them? We certainly can't hunt upland game birds without dogs. But, we could always get a different hobby.

Don't think that I'm forgetting that some dogs do have jobs. There are a lot of service dogs that help handicapped people. These dogs are truly amazing and they are invaluable to their owners. Then there are police dogs that are out there serving a sometimes uncaring public. That's something the police themselves are familiar with. I've even read lately about bomb sniffing dogs working with the military. These are all great things and they show the diversity and talent that dogs possess.

Still, most dogs don't have enough to do. Their potential stays untapped. When someone gets a dog as a family pet, they don't have in mind the ways the dog might help out around the house. The dogs don't usually get a list of chores handed to them. They have no responsibilities other than some token home defense role. That's mostly an honorary thing though. I know of no dogs being fired for letting their owner's house get robbed.

Lack of responsibility is a problem for Weimaraners. People with Weimaraners in their house will have more success if the dogs have something to do. The idle Weimaraner will rampage across the counters and mangle your favorite shoes. Our dogs will find something to do if we don't give them something. And their idea of something to do usually means trouble. It's a never ending struggle to keep these dogs occupied. Dog toys don't work. Any dog toy that gets Grace's undivided attention for an hour is doomed.

So, the dogs seem to get all the tangible benefits and we get more vague things like "the warmth of a cold nose". At least that's better than the warmth of a hot dog butt on a summer evening.

No relationship is all positive. Dogs are a lot of trouble. They are a hungry mouth to feed. They bark at neighbors, mail carriers, meter readers, and family members but not at robbers or salesmen. Unless you have the kind that doesn't get off the couch, dogs have to be walked every day. Weimaraners have to have "their edge" taken off with as long a walk as possible. And I may have mentioned this before, but it can't be complained about enough, owners have to pick up all the poop. I've developed a poop management system that makes it more tolerable. Right now I'm clearing our yard of leaves a little at a time. Each load gets placed in a blue lawn, leaf, and poop bag. And I have become as desensitized as possible. But, I can't imagine a time when I say "Hey, give them extra food so they'll poop even more!"

These dogs have more vet bills than I do. Having a working relationship with a vet is invaluable and almost inevitable with Weimaraners. We've practically got a hotline to our vet. We have to ask questions about injuries because, at some point, you've seen the vet stitch, staple, and bandage a dog enough times to be able to do it yourself. A vet won't tell you to take care of an injury at home if they don't know you and trust that you can handle minor things. And there will be minor injuries with crazy active dogs. There's plenty of chances to hone your vet skills. Our dogs run down hill as hard as they can without ever thinking about how they will stop at the bottom. Grace just skids to a stop. Either they are fearless or they can't think five seconds into the future. Sometimes injuries happen because Weimaraners are over confident. Grace cut her leg open trying to push a car over. Logic should have told her she can't flip a car. But, she didn't use logic, she used her shoulder. Our quick assessment said this one was too bad to fix at home. The vet had to staple her up. None of us actually witnessed this vehicular assault, we just dealt with the aftermath. Post vet visit interviews revealed that Grace was just about to roll the car onto it's top when it reached out and cut her because it knew it was going to lose. I doubt however, that the car was truly, "Asking for it."

People used to be able treat the vet like it's the hospital. You don't go to the hospital unless you have to. I don't go to the hospital unless someone tells me to and I can't say no. But, many years ago more people kept their dogs out in a doghouse than they do today. We've gone soft worrying about these dogs getting cold. Dogs have moved inside and there's probably no going back. With dogs and their dog germs living in the house now, prevention is key.

Vet bills have to be factored in before getting a dog. But no matter how much factoring you do they still pop up unexpectedly. You think you are having a pretty good week and suddenly you have a vet bill for a hundred bucks because your Weimaraner thinks it's bigger than a car.

We know that kids love dogs. And it's apparent that parents buy dogs for their kids even though they know the kids won't take care of it. The parents almost always end up taking care of the dog. I think parents use it as an excuse to get a dog that they wanted in the first place.

Do we need dogs for companionship? Dogs are much easier to get along with than some people. There's a t-shirt that says "The more people I know, the more I like my dog."

Do we have to have dogs just because we are "dog people"? I hear people say this when they're standing in the cold rain holding a leash and asking their dog to hurry up and pee. They don't quite know why they have a dog or why they put up with all the dog baggage. The bottom line is dogs make us feel good.

As easy as it was to observe dogs in my neighborhood, I found that it's not the same everywhere. Sometimes we go to Ocean City for a long weekend. It's nice to get away and these days the town doesn't shut down in the winter the way it used to. So, we'll go any time of year. But, you can see that the place is changing. It becomes less dog friendly every year. This is a town with more dog ordinances than I could count. There are dog signs everywhere but there's a collection of the major dog laws posted on signs near the ocean. The sign is huge, you lose interest before you could finish reading it. You don't have to bring a book to the beach, you can just read the "sign of expected behaviors." The first time I tried reading it I gave up halfway through and thought, "Ok, I get the message." They'd rather you leave your dog at home, but if you do bring it here just know that they can make things uncomfortable for you. A lot of the signs tell you exactly what the fine is for whatever your dog might be doing at the moment. This is handy and helps me to know how much money I need to carry. I let Sadie and Grace off the leash at the beach one time just so I could say I broke fifty laws at once, twenty five per dog. I don't want to give the impression that Ocean City is strict. Judging by the number of people getting run over, there's clearly no problem with getting hammered and walking into traffic. I've never seen any drunk dogs in O.C. but I'm sure there's a fine for it. I don't know if Ocean City is some kind of "city of the future" or if they are just uptight because people on vacation really don't want to see dog poop. Whatever it is, Weimaraners need to walk on egg shells there. Not their specialty.

Whatever sort of neighborhood you live in, free or highly regulated, you can greatly increase your dog knowledge just by getting out and taking a look.

In conclusion, a dog breed is more than just gray fur and floppy ears. The breed is your best guide to successful dog owning. Cuteness should never be a consideration. If you hear yourself use the words cute, adorable, or precious during any part of the dog buying process, start over.

We have dogs today because that's what we want. And we can have what we want until the government tells us we can't have it. But, we'll probably still have dogs because we're just that rebellious. So, don't try it government. We're keeping our dogs no matter what.

Nebraska Again

I headed back out to Nebraska later in 2011. This trip was going to be strictly hunting. No sight seeing was scheduled. Nebraska has wild pheasant, grouse, prairie chicken, and quail hunting. Many people say it's the best in the country.

I was ready to see if I could keep up with wild birds now. My previous attempt in Michigan had left me defeated and shaking my fist at the speedy birds. I had been spoiled by the slow birds we'd been shooting in the game preserves. It was easy to forget that those trips to the game preserve were primarily outings for dog training. The birds in the preserve were much slower than what I saw in Michigan. And they still presented a challenge for me. Even though they were just dry runs meant to get the dogs as sharp as possible, I was using them to improve my shooting. I was now good enough that Sadie didn't give me funny looks anymore. I didn't know how good, or bad, I was. But, I figured it was closer to bad. So far in my hunting experience, the only wild bird slow enough for me to hit were geese. Grouse are on a completely different level as far as shooting skill is concerned. I had no idea what was going to happen with these birds in Nebraska.

What I did know is that what we were about to do in Nebraska was what we had been looking forward to since the day we got Sadie. Training was over, the main event was about to happen.

Mary Ann and the dogs were already somewhere in Nebraska so as usual we met at the Omaha airport. The SUV is easy to pick out of the crowd of cars because it's the only one with two Weimaraner's sticking out of the sunroof. Mary Ann let's them do that for effect only. She knows they will be crazy excited to see me and they have a good view from up there. We never let them hang their heads out the windows with the vehicle moving. Grace would love to catch bugs that way but we think it's a bad idea.

Omaha is a much more interesting city than it gets credit for. It's too far from either coast to get many tourists, and it benefits from it. Most of the people there, live there. I like a town where Mary Ann and I are the only tourists. My first trip there in 2011 was during a massive flood. The view from the plane made Omaha look like an island. There was so much water everywhere I wondered how it would ever get back to normal. The previous winter had seen massive snowfalls in the mountains to the west. When it all melted it had to go somewhere and Omaha was in the way.

The weather was surprisingly warm for early November. I guess it was global warming. Which I don't mind, I just wish it was more consistent. The global warming we have in Maryland is totally unpredictable. We still can't play golf in

January on a regular basis. Some people tell me that I shouldn't make jokes about global warming because it's such a crisis. A really slow moving crisis, but still a crisis. I haven't seen anything that makes me think we can stop global warming. Government rules haven't slowed it down one bit. If it's going to happen, it's going to happen. We might as well make the best of it. If rising shore lines and temperatures are such totally overwhelming problems that they will kill us all, then I'm going to be very disappointed.

The bottom line for me that day was that I had packed a lot of cold weather gear. Now, it looked like it might be staying in the suitcase. I mentioned before that winter in Nebraska concerns me. I don't want to see my concerns realized. When I see gates on the interstate that get closed because there's too much snow on the road, I get concerned. You could call it a fear of freezing to death. I asked why they don't plow the snow out of the way and people shake their head at me in pity. They tell me I don't understand just how much snow there will be on that road. And I don't, but I can imagine quite a bit. I do not need to see those gates in action. (By the way, the irony of freezing to death on a snow covered highway during a global warming crisis is not lost on me.)

If you want to leave Omaha and stay in Nebraska, you have to head west, so that's what we did. In fact we went way west, all the way to North Platte. Upon our arrival, I discovered that the global warming crisis had not reached this far west yet. Here it was cold, but there had been no snowfall. Locals suggested that the snow could start at any time now. Our choices in hotels were limited both by having dogs and being in North Platte. We were staying in a motor lodge that lived up to it's name. Our standards are pretty low and this place met them. They had a free breakfast that was worth every penny. Surprisingly, on the other end of the motor lodge was the best restaurant in town. This was very fortunate because most nights we were too tired to drive anywhere. Most towns have some hidden gem restaurants that take a while to find. Locals told us that wasn't the case in North Platte. What I remember most about the places we stayed in Nebraska is the spot out back where we took Sadie and Grace to do their business. We end up spending so much time there that it's a stronger memory than some of the towns we visited. This was one of the nicer spots. They had a grassy area that backed up onto a corn field. There was a picnic table where motor lodge employees went to smoke. I often thought I should write a guide to the best places to let your dogs poop in Nebraska. It can be a real problem for travelers and most books ignore it. Sadie and Grace did all the hard research, they pooped all over the state.

Hunting invariably makes me think of Robert Ruark. Ever since I read Ruark's book, Horn of the Hunter, about being on safari in Africa I check to see if I'm having as much fun as he did.

Living in a motor lodge in North Platte is not the same as being on safari in Africa. For one thing, the scenery is not as good. Although, we were daily driving hours south of North Platte into some very nice country. Also, somehow the food didn't seem as good as what Ruark described on his safari. There could be a number of reasons for that. His cook was preparing food that had been shot that day on an open fire. We weren't shooting that much and were too tired after walking for miles to do much more than order out or walk to the restaurant. The motor lodge wouldn't allow us to have an open fire anyway. Ruark had a camp cook. I had an exhausted wife, Taco Johns and Runza. Ruark usually had decent weather, I had the Nebraska winter ready to pounce on me.

However, there were some nice parallels between what we were doing and what Ruark had done. We were getting up in the morning, planning our route and going out to bag whatever nature brought our way. It was similar to Ruark's daily routine. His guide had a plan but Ruark wasn't always aware of what it entailed. One difference was the choice of game. Sure, a pheasant isn't as big a challenge as a leopard, but I'm not nearly the hunter that Ruark was. I don't have any desire to work hard enough to shoot a leopard anyway. However, if I did shoot a leopard I'm positive Grace would try to retrieve it. I can almost see her wide eyed stare and hear her saying, "Get me one of those Ken."

Ruark mentions a number of times in Horn of the Hunter, that bird hunting was his first love. When a hunter wants to take time off from hunting the big game to go hunt grouse, as Ruark does, you know there's something about wildfowl hunting that's special. And I think I see what Ruark saw in it. So, there's no reason for me to think that leopard hunting is better than pheasant hunting. It wasn't hard to realize that I was as happy hunting birds out of North Platte as I would have been hunting lions in Africa.

Another difference between our safari and Ruark's was that he had a professional hunter with him that knew where the animals were. We had a map.

We knew no one in Nebraska that had any land that we could hunt on. So, our plan was to use the public land that farmers and the state set aside for hunting. Mary Ann had obtained the necessary land charts before I got to Nebraska. But, the parcels were too scattered for her to do any real scouting. We were just hoping they were good places to hunt. The first thing I noticed about the fields we hunted was that the cover was so much better than what I was used to in Maryland. I can't quite understand why this would be so. The winters in Nebraska are harsher than anything I've ever seen in Maryland. Last year we didn't get any snow at all. The cover in Maryland just isn't interested in growing. Maybe that's why grouse abandoned the state.

My geographic knowledge was growing quite a bit. Nebraska is divided up into what they call sections. Each section is generally one square mile of land. Most of the public lands were not complete sections nor were they square but many of them had more square yards of land than the hunting preserves we were used to. After traipsing through these fields for a week we came to two conclusions. One was that we had missed the good part of the season. We started hunting in the second week of the season and most of the dumb birds had been shot. The smart ones were hiding. The second thing was that a lot of people had our map. We regularly saw trucks already parked beside land we had planned to hunt. And we saw trucks full of dogs and orange clad people drive by us while hunting. The other possibility is that Nebraska's reputation as a bird hunting paradise is an elaborate ruse to get people out there to spend money at fine Nebraska motor lodges and taco restaurants.

One bird that is doing well and surviving in big numbers is the meadowlark, the Nebraska state bird. The dogs found a number of them and it is lucky that I had Mary Ann in the field to say "meadowlark" or I would have spent all my taco money on fines. I've never eaten a meadowlark but they look just like quail to me and probably make a good sandwich.

I shot zero birds in Nebraska and Mary Ann shot only a few. Mary Ann hit more birds with the SUV than I shot. She did get to shoot a wild grouse over Sadie and a wild quail over Grace. So, those were the highlights as far as birds in the bag. The dogs performance was good. They pointed a number of birds that we couldn't shoot, like hen pheasants. Just try explaining that rule to Grace. She doesn't buy it. She considers those birds missed opportunities. Her answer to every explanation is, "But, it's a bird."

The best looking bird we got was a cock pheasant that we found dead by the side of the road. There was a long discussion about bringing a dead bird along with us. We had two yes votes in the back seat. It couldn't have been dead long. There were no bugs on it and it wasn't even stiff yet. So, we put it in a bag and took it with us. We couldn't eat it but it's feathers might make it onto a fly that attracts a trout that makes it to our frying pan someday. Hint, hint.

We didn't see the number of birds that we had hoped for so we couldn't help being disappointed by Nebraska. We had broken one of our cardinal rules by anticipating success on a hunting trip. That set us up for a big letdown. On the bright side, we were in an area that we had no prior knowledge of and no assistance from locals landowners. That's okay because we definitely learned a lot about Nebraska and hunting on public land. I'm quite sure we made mistakes that would have been obvious to people that live there. That's how it goes when you are hunting. And at least I know I'm really a hunter because I never once thought that I was wasting my time out there. It's a cliche to say the experience is more valuable than what you shoot, but it's still true.

What was so memorable about this trip is the time I got to spend with Mary Ann, Sadie, and Grace. The days were full of new places and sights to see. The nights were full of delightfully tired Weimaraner's that seemed as happy as they could get. We were able to stay a step ahead of the weather. One day the forecast was for 5-7 inches of snow for North Platte. We bought extra provisions and planned to wait it out in the motor lodge. Instead, we ended up hunting for about seven hours that day. Total accumulation was zero inches and I didn't see a single flake all day. I'm not saying God wanted us to hunt that day, I'm just saying that we prayed for good weather and a huge snowstorm went poof, like dust.

We also enjoyed the anticipation of being in fields with great cover that could have held any number of birds. The fact that they didn't seems secondary now. We can take some satisfaction that we did things the right way, using public land that we didn't have to pay a cent to hunt on. I'd like to say something about the Nebraska DNR police but I didn't see a single one the whole time I was there.

In the evenings when we relaxed in our spacious lodgings,

after getting a bite to eat, we talked over the day's hunt and planned our strategy for the next day. These are the kind of nights to savor. There's two kinds of tired. We were the good kind of tired those nights. And, as usual I remember them more fondly now than I did while they were happening. I enjoyed myself immensely in Nebraska but it was only later that I realized how great a time it was.

We'll probably return to Nebraska again someday. But, we'll wait until some rich landowner invites us to stay in their lodge and hunt their ten section farm.

Obligatory Dog History

Dogs are descended from wolves. That seems to be the one indisputable fact about the history of dogs.

At some point in history, wolves and people coexisted in what was probably a contentious manner. It's not hard to imagine that packs of wolves competed with packs of people for the available food. Then these people from what is technically known as the "cave man days", started to domesticate some of the more lazy wolves. Like most important historical events, this domestication occurred before people were obsessed with documentation. And these people were probably not as impressed with themselves as we are today. The typical to-do list back then would have included killing a wooly mammoth with a spear, making fire from a stick, defending the family from attacks by the neighbors, securing and cooking the wooly mammoth, going to Cave Depot, sprucing up the cave, and if you have time, do something about those pesky wolves trying to steal dinner. I can't see activities like writing it all down being very attractive. No wonder it took so long to develop written language. People were just too tired.

Modern people document the smallest details of their lives. It's not uncommon to see tweets that talk about the fascinating lunch they serve at the mall. I'd love to see some tweets from the "cave man days". "Had wooly mammoth for lunch again today. Am so tired of mammoth, just really need a salad once in a while."

Although no-one knows all the details about the way wolves were domesticated, theories abound.

The theory that makes the most sense to me is the one involving snacks. The story goes that a somewhat friendly, or hungry, wolf ventured near a campfire and found the people there willing to share their food. Repeated treat hand outs turned an enemy into a buddy. If that's not exactly how it happened, it's close enough, because as I said, no one knows for sure. The wolf might have been going over to the fire to eat the people and just settled for the snacks. That's very dog-like.

A long and successful partnership was begun that night in front of the fire. Neither side could have known how many animals they would eventually hunt, herd, and cook.

Early dog breeders must have had it tough. The hazards of potential sires that had too much wolf left over are obvious. It sounds like one of the more dangerous occupations for that time. It would be easy for early dog owner's to pick the best breeder because they would be the ones with the most fingers. You can just imagine young kids deciding not to go into the family business. Professions less dangerous than dog breeder included nearly everything.

Here's an early ad for a dog that was found chiseled on a stone. "Mixed breed, doesn't bite too much, terrible with kids, free to a good cave." Early dog owning was an adventure. But, there were a lot less rules. I'd love to try and explain to a caveman dog owner the purpose of a roll of poop bags. Me: You see, you pick up the poop with the bag and throw it in the trash can. Caveman: Throw it in the what?

If Sadie and Grace have any wolf left in them, I don't see it. Sadie can't even go to sleep if she doesn't have a pillow. And Grace likes the central air conditioning set to a cool 72 degrees. Neither dog will go out in the rain when they are sleepy. If they see rain when I open the door before their morning tinkle, they both try to turn around and go back to bed. "Never mind, we'll pee when the rain stops." They seem more like British butlers than wolves at that point. They'd choose a little discomfort in exchange for not having to get their feet wet first thing in the morning. This kind of sleepy behavior doesn't last long. After they have time to wake up they turn into happy puddle jumpers. Still, it's not very wolfish.

The wolf connection is something dog's used to be proud of. In the past it probably seemed like a good idea to have ancestors that were known to be mean and edgy. It meant that you were mean and edgy and that's kind of cool. But, the prevailing public opinion doesn't like mean or edgy. Current trends are going against wolf links. Many people want nice, bland dogs these days.

Every book about Weimaraners attempts to include a chapter on the history of the breed. But, a bunch of speculation isn't really a history.

I included the true history of Weimaraners in this book. That definitive chapter stands alone as the secret truth. The commonly accepted history of Weimaraners is quite different but is built on a nearly equal lack of evidence. That lack of evidence allows us to proceed with all manner of speculations. In the interest of space, I've distilled the history down to the bare bones.

Every history of the Weimaraner mentions Karl August. He was the Grand Duke of Weimar in the early 1800's and a hunting enthusiast. The legend says that the grand duke gave Weimaraners to the people he favored in his court. He appears to have had the market cornered on Weimaraners. These dogs don't seem to have existed anywhere else in the world at that time. But, maybe somebody was better at keeping secrets than August.

There are descriptions of dogs that match Weimaraners going back much earlier. And it seems likely to me that the development of a distinct breed of dog would take longer than one grand duke's lifetime. So Weimaraners, as a breed, would be much older than the Grand Duke's court. How then, could August become the only source for Weimaraners in the whole world? I don't know. And I'm not a dog breeder. But, I have met dog breeders and they don't know either. That means the floor is open for wild guesses.

Many people think that all modern hunting dogs are descended from the Saint Hubertus Brache. The Brache was a black hound dog that is extinct now. It does not seem likely that the Grand Duke could have started with Brachen and ended up with Weimaraners. That work must have been started by someone else. Whether it was done by older members of the August family or someone else is another mystery. The Grand Duke may have started out with some dogs that were reasonably close to modern Weimaraner's and did some selective match making. This could have given us the dog we have now. I've always thought that this theory seems too "hands on" for most royalty. So perhaps it would be better to say that the Grand Duke was the program administrator, or, the program was run at the behest of the Grand Duke.

If Karl August really did develop Weimaraners as the breed we know today I wish he had spent some time getting rid of the white spot that some Weimaraners have on their chest. I have no idea if this is possible or what the logistics of this request would entail. But, it would have saved a lot of people a lot of heartburn. I don't see what the big deal is about white on the chest. Every book I've read says that ideally, it would not be there. So, it's a flaw. Only a small dot is acceptable. Grace has a white star shape on her chest. I've told her many times it is not acceptable but she doesn't care. She's not about to acknowledge someone else's idea about how she's supposed to look. But, what if she did? What if she was capable of an inferiority complex? Can you imagine the therapy bills?

It seems like the Grand Duke and his merry band of Weimaraner breeder's either forgot about the white spot or didn't care about it. If they forgot then this is an oversight that shows lack of attention to detail. If they didn't care about it then what is all this "flaw" talk?

The Weimaraner developers could have shown more foresight. They could have predicted people fighting over puppies with no white spot on their chest. Of course, none of them are around to answer these questions. That was probably part of their plan all along.

Modern people like us have to keep in mind that things were different in the nineteenth century.

It's not difficult to see how Karl August was able to keep the existence of his Weimaraners a secret. The world was bigger back then. We tend to think that communication was always like it is now. Or, we think it was better than it really was. There was no one tweeting about the new Weimaraner litter or sending pictures out on their cell phone. They didn't even have landline phones. In fact, they didn't have a reliable way to send a letter. So, when some piece of news went "viral" it meant the people one farm over heard about it a few weeks later.

Weimaraners probably roamed the countryside, hunting and having fun like they do now. Perhaps even fraternizing with their wolf friends. But, even in the city of Weimar most people had probably never seen or heard of Weimaraners. So, it wouldn't have been difficult for someone as wealthy and influential as a grand duke to keep his hunting dogs away from the public.

The real mystery is why the "nearly" Weimaraner dogs didn't exist in other places in Europe. If the breed is as old as it apparently must be, it must have had time to spread to places outside Germany. It seems likely that good hunting dogs would have been valued and kept in any number of countries. And they would certainly have been called something other than Weimaraner.

The kind of evidence that we need to prove that Weimaraners existed is a drawing or painting of one. We need definitive artwork that truly shows a Weimaraner outside Germany before Karl August's time. I haven't seen any evidence of that artwork. There are a lot of paintings of dogs that supposedly show Weimaraners but, they don't look anything like modern Weimaraners. Most of these dogs would be slapped down by the AKC for snipy muzzles.

And there's no sense in blaming the artist. Many of these paintings are very good. There's no reason to believe they didn't faithfully depict the dogs they saw. They did a good job on the people so lets not malign their artistic skills. Weimaraners are naturally attractive to artists. It's hard to believe they wouldn't have been the subject of some study in grayness.

That's the history and latest speculation of Weimaraners as it stands today. You may say, "That's pretty thin." And it is. Further development of the history awaits the discovery of secret documents from the Karl August archives. Without these documents, which may not exist, there's very little we can do except sit around and talk about what we think may have happened. That's more fun than having the whole history spelled out for us.

Horn of the Hunter

I've mentioned that I used the Internet to learn about hunting. The Internet is quick and there's a certain volume of information there that can be valuable. It's not as useful as walking around in the woods. But, you can pick up things by reading what other people are saying. On the other hand, listening to a thousand voices at once can be confusing. And it can be very loud. I wanted to read a book about hunting and enjoy the relative quiet of listening to one voice for a while.

A book would allow me to focus on one person's hunting experience. Listening to a single voice for four or five days seemed like it would give me a better picture of how a hunter looks at the world. Of course, it would have to be the right book written by the right hunter. I wanted to start out reading someone's memories of hunting, since I didn't have many of my own. I didn't want to read a history book or a how-to guide. There would be plenty of time for that later. Right now I just wanted to listen to someone talk about their hunting trip.

I don't consciously collect books. They just seem to pile up around me. I've been reading books continuously since I learned to read. I never stop and usually I have more than one going at a time. It's not a problem to read two or three books at once. You just have to learn to choose the right books. I can't read two novels at the same time. But, I can read a novel, a history book, and a political book without getting them confused.

As I started to collect information about hunting, there was one book that I heard mentioned repeatedly. Horn of the Hunter by Robert Ruark was often referred to as a classic hunting memoir. Ruark himself was revered by some of the people that wrote for the big hunting magazines. I quickly settled on Horn of the Hunter as the first book I wanted to read about hunting. And just as quickly I learned it was out of print. I couldn't find a copy anywhere on the Internet for a price that I would pay.

This made me think two things. Maybe this book wasn't as good as everyone says and maybe I've become totally spoiled by buying books on the Internet. A lot of great books go out of print so no judgment should be made based on this state. It's more a comment on the sad state of reading in the world than it is on the books.

The greatest thing the Internet has done is make more books available to me at low prices. It was supposed to do bigger things like "free China" and "save the planet" but so far it has just made shopping really convenient. The experience of not being able to get a particular book is rare these days. I had to resort to going back to used book stores. I realized that I hadn't done this in years and a few of the stores I used to go to were gone. More casualties of the Internet age.

So Horn of the Hunter was not destined to be the first book I read about hunting, but it has been the best one I've read so far. The pictures I had seen of the cover show a drawing of a cape buffalo. I had somehow gotten it in my head that the horns of this cape buffalo were what the title referred to. How clueless was I?

The horn Ruark is talking about is the one hunter's hear calling them into the field. The one that sparks memories of the way our ancestors lived. Back when we had to get our food directly from the field instead of from the store.

I knew nothing about Ruark himself when I started the book. There's always the chance that you won't like someone once you get to know them, but Ruark was someone that I needed to know, one way or the other. I saw his name mentioned in the same sentence with Ernest Hemingway. So, I mistakenly thought that his writing would be like Hemingway's. I suppose no one writes like Hemingway, but I prefer Ruark. His writing is more accessible and much funnier.

Ruark was a journalist and a hunter. He wasn't a hunter that decided to start writing so he could write off some trips on his taxes. Writing and hunting were a big part of who Ruark was.

I shouldn't have been surprised that his writing style was enjoyable. Clearly, many people have loved his work. But, when you are expecting Hemingway and you get Ruark, it's a happy surprise.

Ruark has such a comfortable writing style that the pages fly by. His descriptions of the land, the animals, and all the things they did while on safari in Tanganyika make for fascinating reading. And they made me wish I had been there.

Ruark's safari is the kind of adventure that most of us will never get to take. The places are so exotic and the very notion of "going on safari" is something hunters dream about. The book is a sort of time capsule. Like all the best books, it captures the unique time in which it happens. Not only does he describe the places they visited, he catches the way the people talked and lived. These things are gone now, they only live on the pages Ruark wrote.

He uses language with a well practiced ease. Hundreds of journalistic assignments allowed him to find his "voice" and he uses it to great effect.

Although he grew up in North Carolina, Ruark is clearly influenced by the British. He spent time in London during World War II and it seems to have had an impact on him. The way he writes sounds British to my ears. It was a surprise to me when he mentioned North Carolina. However, this may be an illusion. It's possible that the American's of Ruark's time sound so different than we do today that I mistake his turns of phrase as being British.

Amazingly, Ruark says that before this safari, he had never hunted with a rifle. I don't think I would wait until I was actually in Africa, on a safari, to break out the rifle. But, he seems to have done okay, it's probably a mistake to second guess him.

We can never take a safari in 1952. So, it's invaluable to have a book that does such a good job of telling us what it was like.

Ruark didn't hunt with dogs in Africa. He could have since he and his wife did some bird hunting while they were there. But, the logistical problems of transporting dogs to Africa are obvious and probably not worth it. However, I'm waiting for the day I hear Mary Ann say, "Hey let's take Sadie and Grace to Africa, it'll be fun!"

Ruark didn't get to do as much bird hunting as he would have liked. His hunting guide was, quite reasonably, focused on big game and didn't want Ruark upsetting the countryside by blasting away with a shotgun. From the way he describes it though, you didn't need a dog anyway. There were huge flocks of birds there. He just sat down in some long grass and waited for them to fly by.

Although I loved the book and will read it many times, it didn't give me much insight into hunting with dogs. What it did give me was a good look at hunter's that were not self conscious or naive about what they were doing. Hunting was as natural to Ruark and his guide, Harry Selby, as breathing. They were hunters for many reasons. And they weren't afraid to say that one of the reasons was because it's fun. They hunted to keep the hunting party fed. They hunted to help out the local villages with their leopard problem. They hunted for trophies. And they hunted for fun. Ruark is completely untouched by political correctness and it's so refreshing to read that it can be stunning. He's unapologetic in his enthusiasm for hunting. These days it feels like we have to justify every bird we kill. Are we more enlightened than Ruark? No, of course not. We might have a wider historical perspective than he did because he wrote this book sixty years ago. But, Ruark knew more about life than a lot of us. He served in the Navy in World War II, travelled over most of the world and spent most of his life writing about the things he'd seen. He knew shooting a trophy animal and hanging it on the wall was a way of immortalizing it. It doesn't demean it or exploit it. Ruark knew that hunting is not wrong. That's not knowledge we've gained, it's wisdom we've lost.

Today, when we talk about preserving the tradition of

hunting, we're talking about doing the same things that Ruark did. Even in his time, the need to hunt to survive no longer existed. He hunted because it is a natural thing to do. But, it's a skill that we need to use and protect or we'll lose it.

We don't need to go to Africa to help preserve the tradition of hunting. There's plenty we can do right here at home. Hunting always seems to be under attack by people that don't like it or understand it.

Ruark himself is also part of the tradition we're preserving. His safari, and the ideas he espoused in his book, are something that need a wider audience. These ideas will help us to stay closer to our roots and keep us from being led astray by those that think our traditions should be abandoned. When we go out to the field to hunt birds with our Weimaraners, we're doing what people have always done.

We've had a lot of political correctness drilled into our head by American society in the past sixty years. And we all have different levels of success in fighting against it. But, we have important examples like Ruark's Horn of the Hunter to show us the right way to think about hunting.

Standard of the Weimaraner

When you live with Weimaraners, the subject of dog shows will inevitably come up. Somebody always looks at these dogs and thinks they are stunning. And so the talk starts that maybe Sadie and Grace could win a dog show. I have been instinctively against the idea of entering a dog show. I've never considered it a viable option for our already limited spare time. And not just because it looks like a lot of running. I was convinced that Weimaraner's should stay out of dog shows completely by the warnings I had read about ruining the breed. I certainly didn't see any value in contributing to that. Even if I didn't completely understand it. Dog shows bad for Weims. Got it. But, I've since learned that it can be done responsibly. So, assuming that something good comes from it, Weimaraner's can have my blessing to participate in dog shows, as long as they hunt as well.

But, there is a problem with dog shows. I'm not exactly sure what they are supposed to be. When I watch that big dog show on TV I'm not comfortable for some reason . I'm not sure if it's a show, some kind of ego trip for the handlers, or sports. It's a competition for sure. The handler's running around with their dogs have a lot invested and are trying very hard to win. No way do I see myself doing it. Running around in a suit while Sadie or Grace do no more than walk fast beside me doesn't sound like fun.

I enjoy watching the dog show but I don't tell anyone that I watch it. I'd be more comfortable with it if it were sports. I've tried to make that stretch with unsatisfying results. I consulted my panel of "experts on all things" in hopes that I could get dog shows included in the pantheon of sports. Ask any group of guys if a certain activity is a sport and you will get a number of different answers and an interesting discussion. I once heard two guys argue for eight hours over whether bowling is a sport. I was captive to this exercise in sport logic and couldn't get away from them. When they finally rested their cases and looked to me for final judgement, I concluded that both of them were right if they would agree to shut up.

Never look in the dictionary or on the internet for answers to questions like this. Too much knowledge and precise definitions will just end cool arguments prematurely. And if someone has brought beer to the argument then the party is over before it starts.

It seems that every attempt at a definition of sport has exceptions. So, one is tempted to just include everything, even dog shows. But, it can't be true that everything is a sport. It's only fun if some things are excluded.

I'll give you some examples of our attempts and you can

add yours at the end. One school of thought is that there are only three sports, football, baseball, and hockey. All these sports require helmets because of the inherent danger of getting hit in the head really hard. When it was pointed out that some sports like soccer and rugby have a high degree of head danger the answer came back, "I'm talking about American sports."

In the end we couldn't agree on exactly what qualities are included in all "sports". But, I did notice that my notion of "sports" is purer and more well thought out than anyone else's. And no two people think of sports in the same way. So the door remains open for dog shows, at least a crack.

Amid all the debate about sports I discovered that dog shows serve a vital function. These dog shows help people keep track of the traits that make a particular dog a Weimaraner. This is important, even if it's on a level that doesn't need to include me. If we don't know what a Weimaraner looks like then soon the breed will become watered down and eventually lost. Some people dismiss this notion as dog show snob nonsense. But, it isn't.

The Weimaraner owner's of today didn't have a hand in the original development of the breed. We have been handed this fine dog and we can either preserve it as it is or we can screw it up. If you know a Weimaraner then you know that they are worth preserving.

There is a certain set of characteristics that, when added up, equal a Weimaraner. That's the standard of the breed. Since we want Weimaraners to be around forever we need a group of people that will breed dogs with this standard in mind. Weimaraners are lucky that there are a bunch of people dedicated to doing exactly that. So, I don't have to worry about it because I have no idea how to breed dogs. Well, that's not exactly true, I'm sure I could get two dogs together, let nature take its course, and make more dogs. Making good Weimaraner's is more complicated than that. To make sure we keep making good quality Weimaraners, I support groups that are concerned with maintaining the traditional form of the Weimaraner. My support is mainly financial. Okay, my support is completely financial. I send them money. But, I keep my eye on them. It's a great luxury to be able to do my part by sending money because if the groups didn't exist, or lost their focus, I'd be forced to take a more active role. And believe me, no one wants that. If amateurs like me take over, Weimaraner's are in trouble.

I'd prefer to go hunting with Sadie and Grace than go to a dog show or hunt test. Plus, I already have too many hobbies.

However, it's only natural to be curious to see if a certain two dogs I know are anywhere close to the standard. I had to know if I was harboring a couple of prize show dogs here at the house.

While reading the standard of the Weimaraner breed that is published by the American Kennel Club, I see why they need experienced judges. There are more things to look at on a dog than I had realized. And a lot of them are small.

The standard also had me reaching for a dictionary. Among the terms that I need some help with were: trumpets, flews, withers, snipy, stifles, hocks, and occipital bone. Sure, I could guess and get close with some of these words, but if you asked me where the flews are, I'd say "Somewhere on the dog, maybe on the upper half?"

Not only were there words I needed to brush up on, there were many descriptions that aren't, for me, intuitive. For example, this comes from the Body section, "The brisket should extend to the elbow." Using my sample dog Grace, I had some initial trouble locating the brisket. What passes for an elbow on a dog was easy enough to guess. It seemed to me that Grace's brisket was riding a little high. Maybe I didn't know exactly where the brisket was located, but nothing seemed to extend to the elbow so I felt safe in saying the brisket didn't either. This was strike one against her right out of the gate. I immediately started questioning the standard. They are telling me that brisket placement is vital? How so? I was ready to throw the standard out and I had just started the canine evaluation. At this rate, Grace might not meet any of the qualifications. I already knew she was too tall. But, I wasn't telling her that. She's slightly sensitive about her height.

This description of the brisket location had me going back to William Denlinger's book, The Complete Weimaraner. This old book has some nice diagrams about various parts of the Weimaraner but nothing to help me with the brisket.

The AKC standard is very detailed while leaving great room for interpretation. In other sports this is the cause of a great many heated discussions. It's the reason baseball fans can't agree on what a "strike" is after playing the game for over a hundred years.

I'm amazed that anyone can judge all these details without carrying a book around with them. Something tells me judges wake up in the middle of the night saying, "Wait! I forgot about the brisket!" I've watched that woman on the TV dog show evaluate pooches very quickly and she's either a genius or she's faking it a little. It's rare that she even takes an extra look at a moosh.

This just shows that I wouldn't be a good dog show judge. Judges put up with a lot of grief from owners of sub-standard dogs. People always think their dog is better than it is. And I'd likely be really bad and honest. That would only add to the grief.

I've looked at a lot of pictures of Weimaraners at shows and after two minutes they all start to look alike. My judging would degenerate into something like this, "That's a Weimaraner, next..." But, my lack of skill and experience isn't going to stop me from seeing just how close, or how far, Sadie and Grace are from the standard. We might end up finding out that they aren't Weimaraners at all. They might be some kind of Weim-like quasi dog.

At first this exercise seems elitist and snobby. The key is in not taking it too seriously. You must answer this question before you start: Is there something "wrong" with my dog if it doesn't meet some aspect of the standard? If a poor score is going to change the way you look at your dog then don't let anyone judge it. Don't even judge it yourself. The standard is an ideal. It's a mental exercise. It's a reminder that keeps us from forgetting what a Weimaraner is. It's not supposed to show you what is wrong with your dog. If some dogs adhere very close to the standard, that's great, give them a ribbon and let's all go home. But, remember that there is no perfect dog.

Now, let's go through some of the more interesting parts of Standard for Weimaraners.

The first section is 'General Appearance'. It states that the Weimaraner should have fine aristocratic features. Then it says the conformation should indicate the ability to work with great speed and endurance. So, the dog should at least look like it can work a field. It should look fast. It doesn't have to be fast.

What exactly does "fine aristocratic features" mean? I've never seen a Weimaraner that didn't have "fine aristocratic features". But, I have seen some aristocrats that look like dogs. So, that seems like an easy box to check for Sadie and Grace. That brings up an important point in looking at the standard. It's all about looks. This isn't a field trial. To Grace's great displeasure, there are no birds at a dog show unless they're on a sandwich. The best show dog may be a great hunter or it may never have found a single bird. It doesn't matter. Sadie and Grace both get a pass in this section.

The height section says that the dog should stand 23-25 inches at the withers, for female dogs.

Sadie is right in the range. Although I measured her while she was asleep. I think that's ok, I didn't get any kind of guide book with my standard. Grace declined to be measured for this category. And it says that a Weimaraner one inch high or low "should be penalized". Not "will be" penalized, just "should be". And it doesn't say what the penalty will be, if there is one. Between you and me, a one inch allowance wouldn't help Grace anyway. Since I'm the judge, I'm not penalizing Grace for this, although I "should" have.

The "Head" section has a number of phrases begging for a flexible interpretation. It calls for a rather prominent occipital bone and "trumpets well set back." Let's see, the occipital bone is on the dog's head. Grace has a thicker than normal occipital bone. She recently took an SUV door to the occipital bone and shrugged it off. Don't worry though, the door is okay.

Then the standard says the flews should be delicate at the nostrils. And I'm sure that is important when the flews are really being tested during a hunt.

I see that there is a lot of leeway in head judgment. With descriptions like "rather prominent", "delicate", "approximately", and "set well enough" you get the idea they want to include as many dogs as possible here. Or they want to be able to exclude any particular dog. Anytime you see the word "moderate" in a description you know it's not a strict measurement. I'd love to know if any dog has been disqualified for indelicate flews.

We have a problem with the ear measurement. It says here that when you pull the ear snugly along the jaw, it should end approximately two inches from the end of the nose. Sadie's ears are closer to the tip of her nose than two inches. Does that mean her ears are too big or her moosh is too short? Grace's ears are farther away. Does that mean her ears are too small or her moosh is too long? But, it says "approximately", and one inch is approximately two inches in some cases. I'd say the size of Sadie and Grace's ears get a pass, approximately. But, are they long and lobular like they should be? Long, yes, way longer than mine. I'm just not sure I can locate their ear lobes. These ears appear to be all lobe. I've decided to do this without looking at the Internet so I'm going to say yes, their ears are sufficiently lobular. And I know these ears work. They can hear a treat bag crinkle at fifty feet in a strong wind. Although again, these ears just need to give the appearance of great hearing. I'd think the bigger the better. But, what do I know?

The Weimaraners expression should be kind, keen, and intelligent. I wouldn't go so far as to describe Grace's expression as kind. It's keen and intelligent all day long, but kind? Her expression actually changes very little, it's placid like a lake on a calm morning. She never snarl's, because she doesn't get mad. The things that would make an ordinary dog mad just puzzle her. When someone defy's her, she seems to wonder, "How could this possibly be happening to me? And why is this peasant being so unpleasant?" And of course she projects her superiority with the push, not by getting mad.

The Body section is the vaguest yet. It uses the term "moderate" twice, the judge’s best friend. This is where the brisket description is located. I mentioned Grace's high brisket earlier but already there's been a dispute about that judgment. A certain co-owner described it as "crazy", although she may have been talking about the judge. This was my first taste of the harsh and unreasonable criticism a dog judge faces. Here I am trying to do my best to be impartial with my own dog and my co-owner lashes out at me. I have to press on even in the face of this angry mobster.

This section includes the phrase "ribs well sprung and long". I've given this more thought than it deserves just trying to decide exactly what it means. But, it doesn't exactly say anything. I'm going to say Sadie and Grace both have well sprung rib cages but again this is where my inexperience shows. I've never seen a Weimaraner that didn't have well sprung ribs. The old saying that goes, "You'll know it when you see it" applies here.

Here's where we try to answer the all important question "What color is a Weimaraner". The "Coat and Color" section is one of the most difficult to judge. Most Weimaraner “owners” will say "gray" when you ask them the magic question. Ask ten people that haven't thought about it and you'll get ten different answers. I asked a Weimaraner owner the question this morning and, unsurprisingly, she said "gray". But, I think she was just saying that because she didn't want to hear me start grousing. I have decided that my answer to the question is "I don't know". The standard says mouse-gray to silver-gray. I've seen a lot of mice that weren't gray at all so I find this description vague. But, believe me I don't envy anyone that has to define these dog's coat.

A Weimaraner's coat is their most unique physical feature.

It's striking and it's what attracts the attention of casual observers. I've written most of this book with a Weimaraner coat within arm's reach and it resists a one word answer. If you look at it closely you'll see that the hairs are not all the same color. This combination of colors gives them a different look depending on the angle and the light. It's the shimmer in the light that makes them look gray.

Any description of their coat will have to include the word "shade". They are a shade of something that might be gray in certain light. It's more like a shade of light brown in some spots and even lighter brown on the undercarriage. Sadie definitely has grey on her head. But, there's not enough of it to call her a gray dog. She's a shimmery dog. If she had that gray hair all over she would look very different. Grace wouldn't allow a close inspection of her coat and said, "Hey stop looking at my head!" I have to inspect her without her knowing it. This isn't difficult considering she comes over to push me a few times every hour.

This section is where long haired and blue Weimaraners get kicked out of the reindeer games. The AKC standard from 1953 calls either of these a "most undesirable recessive trait." Which is true I guess, at least from a technical standpoint. If you take the position that the Weimaraner wasn't "supposed" to have those traits from the very beginning.

Can the standard change? Yes, it has changed several times over the years. There were some minor changes in 1971. Some of the language was clarified. Dewclaws had been optional on the forelegs but were now to be removed. And being oversized was not previously a disqualification. Now the tall dogs are out, sorry Grace.

If it is truly a standard then it shouldn't change very often. If you start hearing people talk about "this years standard" then you know the club is straying from the important things. The AKC standard hasn't changed in forty years. So they can't be accused of flip flopping around. The point is that the standard can change if there's a good enough reason to do so.

The Weimaraner Club of America uses the AKC standard and their stance on blue Weimaraners is in accordance with the German Weimaraner club. The Weimaraner clubs in most countries seem to defer to the German club's rules because it's seen as the "original". The blue controversy rages to this day and isn't going away because there are more and more blue owners that feel their dog should be included. And they use ever more scientific arguments to make their case. The blues even have their own club. I'll never be able to get Sadie into the blue club. Grace might have a chance if she's been painting.

Long haired Weimaraners are odd looking to someone that looks at short haired Weimaraners all day. The AKC doesn't like long haired Weimaraners. So, maybe they need to spend more time looking at them. The AKC standard does not agree with the German standard on long-haired Weimaraners. In Germany and other countries, the long-haired Weimaraner is accepted.

The "Foreleg" section says that the legs should be long and straight. I guess it's important to check that the dog in question has straight legs. But, it seems like an obvious point. If your dog has crooked legs and you enter it in a dog show then it isn't the dog that has the problem.

In the "Hindquarters" section, we learn that Weimaraners should have "well angulated stifles." "Well angulated stifles" means whatever the judge wants it to mean. In my case I've judged Sadie and Grace's stifles to be well angulated. And maybe very well-angulated in some cases. Again, it may be a mistake to do any judging while the dog is taking a nap, but again, I don't have a guidebook.

Sadie and Grace have webbed feet, just as the "Feet" section says they should. I'm sure this is to help them swim and is the reason I will never try to race them in the water.

Continuing on our tour of the Weimaraner we arrive at the "Tail" Section. All tails must be docked. A non-docked tail on a Weimaraner is a weapon. If you have any doubt that docking their tails is a good idea then you haven't been hit in the shins enough. Or had all your tables and shelves cleared off by a rogue tail. Initially, I thought the fact that having their tails docked can hurt was a reason to not do it. However, docked tails make co-existing in a house with a Weimaraner possible.

Believe it or not there is a section in the Standard called "Gait". Essentially, Weimaraners should be able to walk without looking goofy. Weimaraners have this little trot that makes them look like they are gliding across the ground. It's clear that this is the way they were meant to move. It's so cool to watch them go from a kind of awkward walk to this graceful glide. When they are taking up all the space on the couch I wish they didn't have such long legs. But, you can see that their legs are perfect for covering the ground they need to while hunting. Sadie trots with her head up while Grace usually has her nose to the ground. This is so I can easily tell them apart when they are fifty yards away.

The "Temperament" section says the temperament should be "friendly, fearless, alert, and obedient." Well, that's close. Two out of four isn't bad. Grace will tolerate you if you insist on being friendly, but it's not her preferred way of dealing with you. Sadie is friendly enough for both of them. Maybe we could enter both dogs and have them take an average. If these four traits are all the judges are looking for, they will find them. If they start taking points away for extra temperament we might be in trouble.

The entire "Fault" section seems to be a list of major insults to use on other dog owners. I've never actually heard any of these descriptions used to describe someone else's dog, nor would I use them myself. But, it's not hard to imagine it happening. Not only do they list doggy bitches and bitchy dogs, they talk about bad teeth, back, coat, feet, ears and snipy muzzles.

I'm breathing a sigh of relief here that they didn't list extreme pushiness. One of the very serious faults is white, other than a spot, on the chest. Grace has that white star on her chest. I can't seem to make her understand that the Standard doesn't like her star. She's kind of proud of it.

There are only three things a Weimaraner can get disqualified for and one of them knocks out Grace. I'm not happy about this regardless of whether she ever enters a dog show. She's only a little bit too tall. I'm just lucky that I don't want to show her anyway. If there is one place that the standard could change it would be in this disqualification section. The long-haired Weimaraners have a great case to make for being included. Other clubs don't disqualify long hairs because it has been proven that two short haired Weimaraner's can produce a long haired puppy.

The owner's of blue Weimaraners face a more uphill battle because no club accepts them. But, who knows, they might one day. And if blue Weimaraners get accepted then maybe real tall Weimaraners will too.

Sadie and Grace do okay in most of the standard categories. Grace is even a little shorter if I measure her while she's lying on her side. So, a reasonable judge that has been drinking might let her slide in the height category.

The judging has to be very picky because most Weimaraners are going to be roughly the same dog. If the judging isn't picky and slightly subjective then sub-standard dogs might slip through and in a few years Weimaraners might be no better than Labs. It's clear that, once the judging gets picky, Sadie and Grace wouldn't win a dog show. Initially, that's disappointing, but I quickly realized that the ego's around here are big enough already, including mine. So, we don't talk about those things. When we say "dog show", Sadie and Grace think we mean hunting shows on TV. They like Ted Nugent and anything to do with elk.

Given the choice between winning a dog show and going hunting for an afternoon, Sadie and Grace would choose hunting and so would I.

When I look at Sadie and Grace and see all the scratches, nicks, and scars they've accumulated over the years running through the woods, I realize it's foolish to think they could win any kind of dog show beauty contest. That's okay with me. I wouldn't trade the memories we have of times they picked up those nicks. Except for the scar Sadie has on her belly from a run in with a barb wire fence. I'd trade that one. And the scar Grace has on her leg from trying to push over a car. Other than those, all the memories are great.

Out and About

Sadie and Grace like to ride in the truck with me but they are terrible co-pilots. I get lost easy and these two won't say anything when I make wrong turns. All I ever hear out of them is "When's lunch?" A GPS seemed like a great idea. In fact, it seems like they must have invented it for me. But, I tried it and I don't like it. It only takes a few minutes for me to start ignoring it. I'd rather be lost than have a little voice telling me where to turn. And the beep option was easier to ignore than the voice. There are a number of benefits to getting lost anyway. Every shortcut I've ever found started with me driving down a road I'd accidentally turned onto. I can almost guarantee that when you go down a road you've never been on, you'll find things that you were wondering about. And it's not like I stay lost forever. I always get where I'm going eventually. Sadie and Grace are more in a hurry. If Grace can get a face full of air conditioning then she's okay for a few minutes. But her head will be on my shoulder before long saying, "You're lost again aren't you?"

When we got our new camper the plan was to use my old truck to tow it. But, it quickly became apparent that I had to get a new truck. The old truck towed the camper a few times and had to be retired. It just wasn't big enough. I got passed by kids on bikes whenever I went up the slightest incline. I had visions of the truck blowing up halfway up a mountain and the camper dragging us all the way back down. Western Maryland has what we call "mountains". They are east coast mountains. If you've seen the Rocky Mountains, the Smoky Mountains, or even the Blue Ridge mountains, then you've seen real mountains. What we have in Maryland are not much more than steep hills. When my truck was so clearly struggling up these hills I felt unprepared. The last thing you should be when camping is unprepared.

The new truck was all about towing. It flies up the hills. When I got the new truck, Grace started eating it right away. She started on all the plastic pieces, knobs, buttons, and anything else that sticks out. I'm sure she'll move on to the seats and doors later. This doesn't bother me the way it used to. I've learned to treat a truck as a consumable. It's not that I don't care how the truck looks but dogs are dogs and I should have known better than to buy a truck with little chew toys sticking out everywhere. Mary Ann threw an empty peanut butter bone into the back seat of the truck, which was a stroke of utter genius. Lately, that bone has been enough to distract Grace during the boring parts of the five minute ride to the farm. It gets stuck down in the door and she can't actually get at it. But, it's enough of a distraction that she gives the truck a break. That's good because now we can keep this truck until the engine wears out instead of getting rid of it because Grace ate so many vital parts that it doesn't run.

When doing errands around town you have to make a command decision about taking dogs with you. On hot days they may have to stay home. Ignore their cries and complaints about unfairness and cruelty. You just can't keep dogs in a hot truck.

The complexity of your errands also plays a part. I don't like to be in a store for over two minutes so I'm not doing all that much on my errands.

Grace likes to go to the feed store. We pick up some pigeon feed, say hello to all the warehouse guys and we're done. It's a quick stop and I don't have to be away from the truck. They've got a store cat there that is the main attraction for the dogs. It's one of the biggest cats I've seen. Grace likes to give the cat an earful of friendly advice. The cat reacts like most cats do, with a yawn. It probably hears trash talk from dogs all day long. I told Grace to leave the cat alone, it probably outweighs her and I'm not sure she could win in a fair fight.

Sadie's favorite place to go is the gas station because so much of her public is there. The station near our house also sells lunch. I always put the windows down while I'm filling up and let Sadie work the crowd. There's a lot of beach traffic in and out of this place. It's a zoo on weekends in the summertime. If Sadie hangs out the window for a few minutes and doesn't get any compliments on her stunning beauty she gets slightly depressed for the rest of the day. It doesn't happen often, she knows what the people over there like.

Obviously, both dogs like to go to the pet store because they can go in and see all the people and food. But, I don't take them in there very often. It violates the two minute rule.

As I said, we get a lot of beach traffic around here in the summertime. The road to the Chesapeake Bay Bridge backs up quickly and for many reasons. I spend a lot of time thinking about how to avoid the traffic. Sadie and Grace think about ways to make me go out in it. Only Weimaraners actually like traffic. Bumper to bumper, stop and go traffic is their favorite. The slower the better. They like nothing better than to have people in other cars admire them. I guess I wouldn't mind the traffic as much if people were waving at me. These drivers seem to love the distraction. I've had people yell at me, "What kind of dogs are those?" I say, "Keep your eyes on the road you crazy maniac." Of course, Sadie and Grace can get away with it, they're dogs. If I waved at all the cars with my tongue hanging out the cops would probably arrest me.

Sadie and Grace got new collars recently. They must not like the smell of new collars because they started personalizing them right away. I turned my back on Sadie for a second and she must have done an alligator roll in something terribly stinky. It's summer and the day was very hot so Sadie was willing to stand still and get hosed off because the water is cool. But she didn't want to give the collar up now that she had it seasoned the way she wanted it. I wasn't sure I'd ever get it clean and Sadie was hoping I wouldn't. Fortunately, this collar is made of sturdy stuff and is as good as new. Until tomorrow, or later today.

That kind of thing is going to happen when you let dogs roam around a farm. There are so many different smells that their noses must work overtime. These dogs are almost all nose. Sometimes I see Sadie put her head back, close her eyes, and just breathe it all in. She looks at me as if to say, "Can you smell it Ken? I'm going to roll in all of it." And she certainly tries to. Grace huff's the air in so fast it's like she's hyper ventilating. Save some air for the rest of us Grace.

Lately, Grace's usual impatience with things has been creeping into her smell rolling time. Instead of getting on her back and rubbing the smell in, she's doing a sort of tumblesault and then moving on. It's like she doesn't want to spend too much time on one smell, especially if she's rolled in it before. She's focused on the future and moving forward. I guess her favorite smell is the next one. I've given up trying to check out every place she does this, but today she was right in front of me and I saw her do a quick roll and keep walking. When I got to the spot I saw the skeleton of a raccoon or maybe a fox. It would have to have been there a long time to be nothing but bones. But I had never seen it despite walking by it nearly every day. I couldn't smell it with my human nose and it must not have smelled very much with a dog nose either judging by the way Grace gave it just a token roll.

I give these dogs credit for changing my mindset on a lot of things. I'm a slow learner and I've come to realize that I'll never know everything at my current pace. One thing that I've finally accepted is to expect the unexpected around here. There was a time when I would have been irritated about having to get half a cow pie out of a dog's ear. I looked at that as something that didn't have to happen. So I resented the time I had to spend fixing it. Not anymore, I've learned to just deal with these things as they come up.

A perfect example, this afternoon we went for a long walk on the farm. We came back home and I'm writing this section in the kitchen while Sadie and Grace sleep it off in the living room floor. I go into the living room for something and discover that one of them has puked up a bunch of grass on the carpet. I didn't hear them do it and have no idea which dog did it. It doesn't matter, just clean it up and move on.

There's no reason to get upset about anything if you expect the unexpected. If you know something is bound to happen you won't be surprised when it does. I'm amazed at how relaxed this attitude has made me. None of it matters anyway, my old self looks kind of uptight to me now. Sure, these things always happen when you are pressed for time. Or when you are out in the middle of Wyoming. Sometimes you will be late for things due to Weimaraners. Sometimes your plans will change because a Weimaraner ripped her toenail off. Sometimes your good shirt will get covered in dog slobber because a Weimaraner got a three inch stick jammed in her back teeth and you had to wrestle it out. Sometimes farmers will get mad because a Weimaraner keeps retrieving chickens. But, that's just how it is. I've found that I like a little chaos in my life and I didn't enjoy it as much when everything was always in order.

I don't see why we can't have Weimaraner TV. It's a channel that would people would love. And I'd actually watch it. They already have a lot of animal shows. Some are good and some are not. None of them have Weimaraners in a starring role.

There are a great number of alligator shows. People don't get tired of watching alligators. I like these shows because I get to watch crazy people try to catch alligators. Also, I get to see places where I'll never get to live. Weimaraners and alligators don't mix. It's obvious that the scenario of Grace trying to retrieve a gator should be avoided.

A quick look at the TV guide shows so many unwatchable channels that it's unbelievable. And someone thought each of these channels was a good idea. I can only imagine the channels that didn't make it. "Paint Drying TV (PDT)" where camera's sit and watch various paint drying. Actually, that could be good if it was done correctly.

I recently took a poll to see how many channels on cable are worthwhile. No one requested this poll, I offered it as a public service. I asked myself which channels have shows that I regularly watch. I found that I don't "regularly" watch anything. And there are only five channels that I ever watch, none of which feature Weimaraners.

Of course, there's the problem of the Weimaraners tendency to get too popular for their own good. The last thing anyone wants is a repeat of the Weimaraner boom of the 1950's. There are already enough non hunting Weimaraners out there. We have to limit the breed's exposure to the public so it doesn't get out of hand again. Weimaraner TV would need a lot of disclaimer's like this one, "Before buying a Weimaraner, take your best pair of shoes outside, place them on the sidewalk, safely chop them in half with your hatchet. If you have no feelings of anger move on to step two of the Weimaraner buying process." Maybe a pay per view channel would keep the casual observer from getting ideas about owning a Weimaraner.

People say "There are millions of videos of Weimaraners on the Internet. Isn't that enough for you?" No, it's not the same because those are mostly clips of someone's Weimaraner doing something interesting. That's great as far as it goes, but I see Weimaraners do crazy things all the time. I'm not saying it ever gets old watching a Weimaraner open the refrigerator and take a midnight snack, but that's more of a reality TV show. What's needed is a fictional show like Lassie, only different.

Sadie the Wandering Weimaraner would make a great show. She'd go to a new town each week solving problems and making life generally brighter. And I have no doubt every network would turn it down flat. That's what the big TV networks do, they turn down good ideas. And they produce shows that follow the same old formula's. That's why they are dying out.

The proliferation of lower budget cable networks has started to chip away at the big network's audience. We are starting to see interesting shows that you'd never see on big networks. Shows that feature people fishing, hunting, going to auctions, buying junk (memorabilia), cooking, building motorcycles, repossessing cars, making duck calls, or hunting alligators would never see the light of day on big networks.

That's why the time for Weimaraner TV has arrived. If Sadie can't be a county councilman because of some intolerant rules maybe she can be a TV starlet. Making TV shows is not something I've ever done. But, apparently you don't have to be good at it to be successful. Just turn on a network show if you want to see how not to do it.

I like to gather as much information as I can so I can ignore most of it. But, going to school to learn how to make movies and TV shows is crazy. It's as crazy as going to a school to learn how to write stories. Starting a school and charging money to show people how to make movies and write stories, now that's a good idea.

Weimaraner TV is such a natural born good idea I'm surprised no one else has had it. What we need is some seed money. Maybe we could have one of those Kickstarter deals. Hmm...

Conclusion

I have a recurring dream that I call "Night of a Thousand Weimaraners". In it I am awakened from a deep sleep by a Weimaraner with a desperate need to go outside. I get up and take her out, she does her business and I go back to bed. No sooner does my head hit the pillow than I am awakened by another Weimaraner with the same desperate request. And over and over and over.

I interpret that dream to mean that my mind has been affected by these dogs at both a conscious and subconscious level. I've been beaten into shape for proper Weimaraner care and feeding. If you told me Sadie just puked up an Oldsmobile I'd start thinking about how I was going to clean it up and if I could still get the car started.

If I could have one wish, it would be for a Weimaraner that doesn't poop. I'm kidding, my one wish would be that people could buy Weimaraner's without seeing them first. If a person could read a description of a Weimaraner, listen to the true confessions of Weimaraner owners, look at their burned out lawns, and still say, "Hey, that's the dog for me.", then they are ready for a Weimaraner. That's easy for me to say, I had a Weimaraner before I could even pronounce it. I'm just aware of how badly it could have turned out and I'd like to spare both the people and the dogs those troubles.

Every Weimaraner is different and every Weimaraner is the same. Your Weimaraner might be great with kids. Sadie loves kids. Grace loves to pin them to the floor with a right paw to the chest. Then she looks around as if to ask, "Whose is this?" Your Weimaraner might be considerate. Grace goes to her kennel to throw up. It's such an easy clean up. Sadie will only throw up in the truck, on the carpet, or on me. And only in the middle of the night or while I'm driving. Your Weimaraner might have gas that smells like fresh flowers. Our Weimaraners could make a skunk leave the room.

Their personalities are unique. They all have their own agenda and will begin implementing it early in life. The common trait is energy. They all have boundless energy, but no thumbs. They need co-conspirators with thumbs. And you are elected.

So, if you didn't get it by now, I'm saying, if you get a Weimaraner and don't like it, it isn't my fault.

People say to me, "Those dogs can't really talk Ken." Yes, I know that but Grace couldn't communicate, "I have to poop." any clearer if she spoke perfect English.

Yes, the versatile hunting Weimaraner makes a fine addition to any home with people that are willing to let the dog think it's their house. These accommodations are a lot of work. But, it's rewarding work.

My conclusion is that Weimaraners make me happy. With so much in the world that doesn't make me happy, I'm sticking with Weimaraners.

27825483R00138

Made in the USA
Middletown, DE
22 December 2015